Jesus Changes Everything

Jesus Changes Everything
A New World Made Possible
Stanley Hauerwas

Edited by Charles E. Moore
Introduction by Tish Harrison Warren

Plough

Published by Plough Publishing House
Walden, New York
Robertsbridge, England
Elsmore, Australia
www.plough.com

Plough produces books, a quarterly magazine, and daily articles on Plough.com to encourage people and help them put their faith into action. We believe Jesus can transform the world and that his teachings and example apply to all aspects of life. At the same time, we seek common ground with all people regardless of their creed.

Plough is the publishing house of the Bruderhof, an international Christian community. The Bruderhof is a fellowship of families and singles practicing radical discipleship in the spirit of the first church in Jerusalem (Acts 2 and 4). Members devote their entire lives to serving God, one another, and their neighbors. They renounce private property and share everything. To learn more about the Bruderhof's faith, history, and daily life, see Bruderhof.com. (Views expressed by Plough authors are their own and do not necessarily reflect the position of the Bruderhof.)

Copyright © 2025 by Plough Publishing House
All rights reserved.

Cover art copyright © 2025 by Julie Lonneman
Frontispiece photograph courtesy of Duke Divinity School

ISBN 978-1-63608-157-1
29 28 27 26 25   1 2 3 4 5

A catalog record for this book is available from the British Library.
Library of Congress Cataloging-in-Publication Data

Names: Hauerwas, Stanley, 1940- author.
Title: Jesus changes everything : a new world made possible / by Stanley
  Hauerwas ; edited by Charles E. Moore ; introduction by Tish Harrison
  Warren.
Description: Walden, New York : Plough, [2025] | Series: Plough spiritual
  guides | Includes bibliographical references. | Summary: "These
  accessible readings will introduce a timely, prophetic voice to another
  generation of followers of Jesus tired of religion as usual"-- Provided
  by publisher.
Identifiers: LCCN 2024027409 (print) | LCCN 2024027410 (ebook) | ISBN
  9781636081571 | ISBN 9780874860368 (epub)
Subjects: LCSH: Christian life. | Christian life--Biblical teaching.
Classification: LCC BV4501.3 .H379 2025 (print) | LCC BV4501.3 (ebook) |
  DDC 248.4--dc23/eng/20240928
LC record available at https://lccn.loc.gov/2024027409
LC ebook record available at https://lccn.loc.gov/2024027410

Printed in the United States of America

Contents

Introduction Tish Harrison Warren		ix
Who Is Stanley Hauerwas? Charles E. Moore		xx

Part I: Following Jesus

1.	Come, Follow Me	3
2.	Far from Shore	7
3.	The Kingdom in Person	11
4.	Becoming Part of Christ's Story	14
5.	Love Is Not Enough	18

Part II: Good News

6.	God's Possible Impossibility	25
7.	Kingdom Promises	28
8.	Be Perfect	33
9.	Subversive Righteousness	39

Part III: God's Alternative Society

10.	God's New Language	45
11.	Living Truthfully	51
12.	A Community of Charity	56
13.	Family and the Church	61

Part IV: Kingdom Economics

14.	What about Wealth?	71
15.	Living on Dishonest Wealth	78
16.	Our Daily Bread	81
17.	On Judas's Side?	84

Part V: Sowing Seeds of Peace

18.	Habits of Peace	91
19.	No Sword but the Cross	98
20.	A Dangerous Business	101
21.	God's Imagination	106

Part VI: The Politics of Witness

22.	The First Task of the Church	113
23.	Jesus Is King	119
24.	Christian Politics	124
25.	The Difference Christ Makes	129

Sources	*134*
Bibliography	*136*

The theologian's task is to make it difficult to be a Christian. It is also to make it equally difficult to be a non-Christian, that is, to present an account of Christianity that shows the difference that being a Christian makes and how that difference may intrigue and challenge those who are not Christian.

—*Stanley Hauerwas*

Introduction
Tish Harrison Warren

STANLEY HAUERWAS feels larger than life. He's funny. He's insightful. He grew up a blue-collar kid in small-town Texas, which lends a grit and plainspokenness to his theological work that keeps us all on the hook. For him, theology is not an abstract game, a jostle amid the experts with their jargon and fashionable truisms, a way to score points against others, or a way to bend the Christian story to fit our preferences. Instead, it is learning the story that teaches us to live.

Because of this, Hauerwas's work has had an unusually important, even intimate, impact on people's lives. I know more than one couple who decided to have children after reading Hauerwas (and I wonder how many men and women Hauerwas will meet in the resurrection who will thank him for inspiring their parents). I – a descendant of dyed-in-the-wool Texans whose ancestral home had an heirloom war rifle hung over the mantel – became a pacifist because of Hauerwas. I have friends who went to seminary to study theology because of Hauerwas's work. His words change people.

Hauerwas is provocative, but not for provocation's sake. Instead, he calls us back to the disruptive words of Jesus, and to the church – to a community of ordinary people who are meant to learn to follow Jesus in the concreteness of our lives in a complex world. He is clear that following Jesus will always come at a cost and will disassemble most of our expectations about how our lives should turn out.

I FIRST CAME ACROSS Stanley Hauerwas's work sometime in the late 1990s, when I was in college. Reading him brought about something like a tectonic shift in my soul. His work changed the landscape. It changed how I saw the world.

I had grown up in a progressive city, Austin, Texas, in the nineties. I was also a Christian who knew about the so-called "moral majority" committed to taking back "family values." In other words, I knew about the culture wars. And I was very cynical about all of it. I certainly never thought God was a Republican or a Democrat. But I didn't know where that left me, and I didn't know how to faithfully navigate American society as a Christian. I had little interest in devoting myself to the political left

Introduction

or right, but I was also uninspired by the idea of being a stubborn moderate trying to walk a centrist tightrope, which seemed antithetical to how Jesus lived his life. (Very few moderates are tortured and executed by empires.) In short, I lacked a Christian political theology and was skeptical of the options the culture (including church culture) seemed to offer.

Hauerwas's insistence that the first social task of the church is to *be* the church oriented me like a lost hiker who discovers a trusty compass. The notion that the church is an alternative community that embodies a different sort of kingdom, and that allegiance to that kingdom is our truest political and social responsibility, came as a breath of fresh air.

Over the twenty years since, as I've grown older, been ordained, and continued to seek to follow Jesus, I've come to see that what it means for the church to be the church is a pretty complicated question. This is why Hauerwas's voice is needed now more than ever. This is why this collection of his writing feels pressing, urgent, and vital. Because Hauerwas's voice is one that helps the church recall who she is and learn how to be the church, even now.

The misguided days of decades past with "moral majority" Christians seem almost quaint now, given the way American politics have metastasized into a vitriolic, quasi-religious conflict. Many Christians see those on the other side of the aisle as their mortal enemies. Yet both the right and the left seem to tacitly agree that the radical calls in the Sermon on the Mount to meekness, mourning, turning the other cheek, and loving enemies are outdated. Some Christians explicitly say that turning the other cheek doesn't work anymore, that we have to fight back now.

But Hauerwas makes clear that turning the other cheek has never "worked," if by "working" we mean creating a nice life for us or for our children that is free of suffering and sacrifice, a life that fits neatly into the cultural expectations and political categories of our moment.

The call of Jesus to, for instance, turn the other cheek and love our enemies only makes sense if it is embodied by a community dedicated to being an embassy of the kingdom of God in wider society. And this will mean that we are, as Paul says, "aliens and strangers." And, whatever else that means, it implies we will never feel quite at home.

For me, Hauerwas is at his most bracing when he says that to deprive Christians of suffering is to tell them that they cannot follow Jesus to the cross. The church today is weak, he says, because of "sentimentality," our unwillingness to allow ourselves or our children to suffer because of our convictions. We use whatever means necessary to avoid the cross.

Introduction

Hauerwas also reminds us that, regardless of political party, any attempt by Christians to grasp control will inevitably give way to a worldliness that devolves into pride and violence. As he says in these pages, the sacrifices required by war and violence are both "counter-liturgies" to the sacrifice of the altar. Jesus' sacrifice on the cross and our participation in that once-for-all sacrifice every time we receive the Eucharist deem the human sacrifice of violence false and idolatrous.

We can be "disciples" of Jesus – rather than mere "admirers" of him – only insofar as we recognize that the story that forms us insists that Jesus is already in control. We don't have to prove this in a show of power or through political means. Instead, we, as a church, are to live into the story of what he's already accomplished on the cross. Jesus – not us or America or the West or democratic politics – has brought the kingdom. Indeed, he *is* the kingdom enfleshed, and he demonstrates this, surprisingly, through his utter vulnerability.

All of this is profoundly countercultural. It's even transgressive. And Hauerwas is, in the best sense, transgressive, not because he's saying something novel but simply because he dares (and dares us) to take the scriptures seriously enough to be disturbed by them. Most of us Christians, particularly in the West, often contort the teachings of Jesus to fit into our own quest for the "good life." We make God our ally in self-actualization and realizing the American dream, and buffer ourselves against the stark consequences of his teachings.

But if transgression in our culture is seen mostly in terms of individuals being "true to themselves," Hauerwas clearly calls people away from individualism and to a specific community. Nothing else Hauerwas says will make sense unless we believe that the church really matters. How we view the church matters. "The church does not have a social ethic," Hauerwas argues; "the church *is* a social ethic." Our ability to welcome the vulnerable, the disabled, and children; to speak truth; to practice generosity; to honor the limits and holiness of human bodies; to live "out of step" with the world; and to love our enemies is the embodiment of an ethic birthed out of the resurrection. This kind of discipleship isn't a strategy for winning an election, having a picture-perfect family, or getting a raise. It is, however, as Hauerwas says, living "with the grain of the universe," and is therefore the strange way of abundant life.

The way the church embodies this ethic is contextual and improvisational. While in some ways "being the church" is a universal and perennial call to all generations, the details and practices of this call will change according to the needs of our neighbors and the failures or strengths of a particular church at a given time. Of

Introduction

course, all of this must be discerned through the power of the Holy Spirit.

What it means for the church to be the church, however, is not to pick a side in the culture wars; nor is it to suss out some moderate position; nor is it to be apolitical or quietist. Instead, we learn together, in conversation with the church throughout time, to embody an alternative community that can approach all of life in a different way, a way shaped by the story and practices of creation, fall, redemption, and consummation.

When Christ came into the world as the king of a kingdom that is not of this world, a kingdom based in truth and not in power, neither Rome nor the Hellenistic civilizations around the church had any categories with which to understand this. Early Christians had no interest in directly supporting or upholding the empire, and they did not participate in the pagan temple sacrifices. In some ways, then, they may seem to have been apolitical.

But, as Hauerwas writes here, the refusal of Christians to kill is what required the church to be political. The early church was interested in a radically different sort of peace than was offered by allegiance to any earthly cause. And this strange political community ended up seeding the world with the gospel.

We, like the earliest Christians, are still called to resist the political categories, assumptions, and demands of our day. What the church does jointly when it gathers for worship is its foremost political action. Proclaiming "Jesus is Lord" has profound (though nonpartisan) political ramifications. We are citizens of another kingdom, called to demonstrate the ethics of that kingdom.

HAUERWAS BOLDLY CALLS US to this vision and charts a path of what it may look like in our own moment and culture. He dismantles Christian nationalism, which seems to be as rampant as ever, yet he also rebukes Christian progressivism and the ways it seeks to make the gospel more palatable to our culture. He calls all of us into something completely different: a community shaped by the cross of Christ, a community that welcomes others without losing itself, a community that makes no sense to this world, because it is formed by the Spirit of God.

Hauerwas also reminds us that as a church we must be formed by a story. In other words, he reminds us that theology matters – that, as he points out, poorly trained Christian pastors and leaders can do as much harm as poorly trained surgeons. In one talk he gave recently, I heard him skewer the oft-repeated truism that "people don't care how much you know till they know how much you care." The church and the pastoral office are being dumbed down so that the pastor is simply a nice counselor or therapist, and the church's job is mostly to make everyone feel happy and uplifted.

Introduction

Hauerwas has no time for this kind of benign faith. (If one is primarily after agreeable spiritual uplift, I'd recommend avoiding Hauerwas.) He insists that we think theologically: that our minds and our whole lives – and our approach to every part of life – be deeply and meaningfully shaped by the story of Jesus. Sit with his words long enough and they become something like a solvent for clichés and platitudes. And this is needed now more than ever. People today often want to reduce the Christian faith to a debate that can fit into a hashtag. But true theology, as Hauerwas brilliantly says here, makes believing in Jesus "more difficult." He understands that we have to struggle to be shaped by the story of Jesus and that if we do not, we will inevitably be shaped by other, lesser stories. Poor theology, then, isn't just some kind of spiritual faux pas. It deforms the church as a community. It produces cruelty and makes the development of Christian virtue impossible. Bad theology makes us into admirers of Jesus, not disciples.

What Hauerwas does well is bring to light the deep logic that is often shared between those who seemingly hold divergent, partisan views. He challenges things we usually take for granted, things like individual autonomy and rights, the idolatry of the nuclear family, the importance of personal identity, and the sentimentality of romance. And, for that matter, the sentimentality of "faith" as well. In challenging the deep logic held by all "sides" in our culture, Hauerwas defies easy thinking and explodes easy answers. He instead insists that Christianity demands a rigor in thought and speech that makes truth-telling possible. Whatever else the words of Hauerwas do, they always make me think – and they teach me to think differently.

HAUERWAS IS IMPOSSIBLE to categorize theologically. He is a Catholic-Anabaptist-Anglican. Sort of. But this is not because he is noncommittal or haphazard about the need for a local church. It's because what Hauerwas offers is the kind of catholic faith that is shaped by a broad tradition of Christian thinking. His vision for the church, then, will challenge everyone.

Hauerwas reminds me that Jesus came to create a people, a polity, on earth. This is part of the gospel. The church is part of Christ's continuing story in the world. And Hauerwas also reminds us that it is always possible – even now – for the church to repent and be reborn. In fact, as he says in this book, this post-Christendom age, when the church is quickly losing status and favor in the West, may be the best time to rediscover what it means to be Christians.

My husband and I often describe our society now as "post-Christendom *and* pre-Christian." This suggests, with hope, that people may be able to hear the gospel

Introduction

anew. It means that God is still after our hearts and the hearts of our neighbors, friends, and fellow church members. As the delusion of an erstwhile "Christian West" fades, and as the number of those reporting no religious affiliation rises, disciples of Jesus may seek to proclaim and practice the gospel without the trappings of respectability, power, political captivity, and nationalism that have so long defined and malformed it. This is a big project, one big enough that it is worth giving our lives to. And in this project Stanley Hauerwas continues to be a key voice helping us chart the way of Jesus – to be the church Jesus created and loves.

Tish Harrison Warren is a priest in the Anglican Church in North America and the author of *Liturgy of the Ordinary* and *Prayer in the Night*, among other books. She was formerly a weekly newsletter writer for the *New York Times*. She lives with her husband and three children in Austin, Texas.

Who Is Stanley Hauerwas?
Charles E. Moore

IN PREPARATION for this book, I asked Stanley Hauerwas if I could look through some of his correspondence. He sent me to the main archives at Duke University and told me, "You can have access to anything. Just tell the librarian I sent you."

When I arrived, the resource librarian told me I needed special permission, which I assured her I had, and that I needed to know that Dr. Hauerwas's papers were extensive and not completely sorted. "Where would you like to begin?" she asked. I thought the years 1985 to 1998 would be a good place to start. Four days later, I had combed through forty file boxes worth of correspondence. Eighty more awaited me if I chose to read further. Hauerwas wanted to know what I had found. I shared a few snippets with him. In feigned astonishment he replied, "I said that?"

Who Is Stanley Hauerwas?

Hauerwas is known for saying things that catch people off guard. It's not that he tries to be provocative, or that he gives new answers to old questions. His desire? To "foment a modest revolution by forcing Christians to take themselves seriously as Christians." That is what this book is about, to challenge Christians about their Christianity by shaking them out of their customary ways of thinking and living, so they can be more faithful to Christ.

In Hauerwas's experience, his writings have often kept people from taking him seriously. "People think my claims are so exaggerated they couldn't be true." Take, for instance, the following statements in this book:

The gospel is about Jesus Christ, not about love.

The worst kind of unkindness is to rob others of their right to suffer.

Some marriages are miserable not because people are not committed to marriage, but because that is their only commitment.

To be rich and a disciple of Jesus is to have a problem.

Following Jesus is never safe.

If we are honest, we find Judas appealing.

The wealth of the church is the poor.

> War is but the desire to be rid of God.
>
> The whole point of Christianity is to produce the right kind of enemies.
>
> Christians are revolutionaries, but we believe the revolution has happened and we are it.

If the above declarations don't catch your attention, or at least make you curious enough to wonder what Hauerwas means, this book is not for you. Though hardly dour, Hauerwas is dead serious. Jesus changes everything! He is not nice, because he actually saves us from ourselves.

BORN ON JULY 24, 1940, Stanley Hauerwas grew up in a working-class home in the small town of Pleasant Grove, north Texas. Starting at age nine, he worked summers with his father, a bricklayer, though he says he never knew he was poor until he left home. He went to Southwestern University, then Yale University, where he received a PhD. He began teaching at the University of Notre Dame before moving to Duke Divinity School and Duke Law School. In the course of his career, he wrote over fifty books. Some, particularly *Resident Aliens*, co-authored with William H. Willimon in 1989, had an impact far beyond academia, changing the way many Christians viewed their role in society.

Who Is Stanley Hauerwas?

Though he has been a prolific author and sought-after speaker, Hauerwas is more than an academic. A committed father of one son, for years Hauerwas quietly carried his first wife's burden of severe mental illness. He treats his students as friends, even jogging partners, and many have indeed become lifelong friends. His commitment and service to his local Episcopal church is unassuming but real. He loves to invite people to midweek Eucharist followed by going out to lunch. His love of life and his laughter are contagious, as is his love of baseball and travel. One can find him working around the house or just walking on campus with students or with a fellow faculty member. Behind the scenes, he visits the sick and sends notes of encouragement to people he knows.

For those unfamiliar with Hauerwas's life and writings, one-liners like the ones I highlighted above may come across as simplistic or overly confrontational. It is true that Hauerwas engages in polemics. But most of his writings are not pithy. In fact, the opposite is the case: they usually consist of extended essays that thoughtfully engage the writings of others at length. Hauerwas is a complex thinker, and to fully appreciate him one needs to read not only his books but also what he has read. If you do, you will find yourself traversing extraordinarily broad intellectual terrain, ranging from political and moral philosophy to theology and practical church issues.

Any attempt to make Hauerwas's work appear more systematic than it is would be a mistake. In this sense, taken by itself this book might be misleading. Hauerwas is indeed forthright, but he is still sometimes hard to pin down. We can see Protestant, Catholic, and Anabaptist influences. This can be frustrating, especially for anyone who wants to "locate" his thought. But it does not mean he doesn't take any clear stands. This book clearly indicates otherwise. It simply means that Hauerwas eludes categorization. He is neither conservative enough for conservatives nor liberal enough for liberals. He is profoundly committed to fundamental Christian convictions while at the same time articulating a socially radical, unnervingly Christian ethic. He is an avowed pacifist and yet sometimes an outright thorn in the flesh.

Despite these juxtapositions, those who read Hauerwas will see repeated themes: the importance of the virtues for understanding the Christian life, the significance of the story of Jesus in determining what it means to be a Christian, the necessity of keeping Christian ethics Christian, the priority of the church as a community necessary for living truthfully, the necessity of nonviolence as an essential mark of being

Who Is Stanley Hauerwas?

Christian in the world, and the deleterious effects of accommodating political arrangements.

On this last point, Hauerwas is most trenchant. His approach to such matters as abortion, euthanasia, war, the death penalty, sexuality, and marriage is a welcome corrective to so-called Christian ethics that are actually guided more by liberal ideals of universal freedom and reason than by Christ. The attempt to do ethics objectively, from "nowhere," has eroded the church's ability to bear faithful witness. "What has to end is the habit of Christians asking non-Christians to do what we cannot get Christians to do." For him, the church, not philosophy, determines what we have to say about Jesus and whether we have anything ethically relevant to show.

According to Hauerwas, the modern story is that we should have no story except the story we choose. We have not only separated ethics from character, but Jesus from the church, pitting Jesus' person against his work and Jesus as teacher against his crucifixion. One can now be a "Christian" without having to become Jesus' disciple. This is like trying to "have the results of the gospel without Jesus." If Jesus had espoused some universal ethic, if his teachings were meant to be attractive to all, he would never have been crucified nor raised from the dead. Any so-called universal ethic is always someone's ethics disguised for *anyone*. Such an ethic either leaves Jesus out or ends up making Jesus, as Kierkegaard described, into our hobbyhorse.

So, what does it mean to bear witness to the Jesus of the Gospels? Certainly not taking control or pushing some "Christian" agenda. Attempts to Christianize the social order in the name of furthering God's kingdom or being politically responsible lead the church to sanctioning war and becoming a perpetrator of injustice. This insight is at the heart of Hauerwas's polemics. That doesn't mean he thinks following Jesus is a matter of holding certain beliefs that are personal and private and religious, or a matter of inner piety. No, following Jesus is "a public affair, with cosmic consequences." To worship him is itself a politics, a politics that subverts the status quo. God has created a world in Christ that otherwise would not exist. That world is called the church.

IT IS TEMPTING to conclude, as one critic has, that Hauerwas's understanding of discipleship demands that we be "sectarian, fideistic tribalists" removed from the world. Hauerwas not only bemoans this mistaken notion but has worked tirelessly to refute it. He is clear that the options before the church are neither sectarian withdrawal nor establishment respectability. Jesus is the kingdom of God in person. He is God's eschatological reality made present, giving rise to a new social possibility called church. On the cross, the principalities and powers of this world are defeated. The cross bears witness to the fact that we don't have to make the world turn out right, nor do we have to follow the dictates of prosperity and power. On the cross, God incarnate refused to save the world by coercion. And neither should we try to. By enduring suffering, God gave us an opportunity to live in the world without killing those who would kill us.

The difference between the world and the church, therefore, lies not in a different set of values or even a different set of means. The difference, simply put, is Jesus. And that is why the first task of the church is to be the church, to be a people that bears witness in its life to God's new creation in Christ. That is not a doctrinal move; it is a political one. "Since Christians cannot kill, politics is a necessity." But this isn't just any politics. It is a politics of hospitality toward the other and toward the stranger, of patience and longsuffering with one's enemies, of caring for the injured and oppressed, and of a peaceableness that is truthful.

Is there anything else this politics of Jesus entails? For one thing, in a world that now lives amid the shards of Christendom, Christians are now free to be Christian.

Jesus Changes Everything

Hauerwas says:

> One of the good things that is happening today is precisely the loss as Christians of our status and power in the wider society. That loss makes us free. We as Christ's disciples ain't got nothing to lose anymore. That's a great advantage because as a people with nothing to lose, we might as well go ahead and live the way Jesus wants us to. We don't have to be in control or be tempted to use the means of control. We can once again live like the first Christians.

And how did the first Christians live? They didn't merely confess Jesus' name but bore witness to Jesus as Lord. That changes everything. They embarked on an apprenticeship to a master through which they learned the skills that made them capable of narrating and instilling the virtues of God's peaceable kingdom – skills that reconcile enemies to God and to each other. This is what enabled the early church to display the kind of world God intends, a world in which there is no longer slave or free, Jew or Gentile, rich or poor, friend or foe. It was a community that in its liturgy and very materiality faithfully told, heard, and enacted the story of God's coming kingdom: the new creation.

To live in *that* kind of world looks strange and, yes, may even appear threatening. Faithful Christians, Hauerwas reminds us, have always been resident aliens.

Who Is Stanley Hauerwas?

And yet they have also always been bearers of good news – not of success or respectability but of the possibility of an alternative society that rejects the dictates of the market and the mechanisms of injustice, power, and violence. This new possibility eliminates the dynamics that pit us against one another – whether politically, economically, or socially – and seeks to fulfill God's will on earth as in heaven.

HAUERWAS USUALLY WRITES dialogically, in conversation with others. This book is different in that respect. It is more straightforward and has a single focus: discipleship. Readers familiar with Hauerwas's work may recognize some of the selections, but he and I have edited them down to get at the heart of what he thinks about following Jesus in today's world.

Be forewarned: this book will quite likely bother you as much as it will inspire you. Stanley Hauerwas and his writings were a large reason why, thirty years ago, I left a professorship at a seminary and moved two thousand miles with my wife to join the Bruderhof, a Christian community that shares possessions in common in accordance with the Sermon on the Mount. Disillusioned with the Christianity we had known, we wanted to live like the first Christians, where no one was in need and everyone belonged.

Jesus Changes Everything

The danger for any follower of Christ is not that we do not believe, but that what we believe does not make any difference, for the church or the world. Hauerwas, both as a person and as a writer, has certainly made a difference. I trust this book will as well.

Charles E. Moore is a writer and contributing editor to *Plough*. He is a member of the Bruderhof.

PART I

Following Jesus

Spirit of Truth, direct our attention to the life of Jesus so that we might see what you would have us be. Make us, like him, teachers of your good law. Make us, like him, performers of miraculous cures. Make us, like him, proclaimers of your kingdom. Make us, like him, loving of the poor, the outcast, children. Make us, like him, silent when the world tempts us to respond in the world's terms. Make us, like him, ready to suffer. We know we cannot be like Jesus except as Jesus was unlike us, being your Son. Make us cherish that unlikeness, that we may grow into the likeness made possible by Jesus' resurrection.

I

Come, Follow Me

Then Jesus said to Simon, "Do not be afraid; from now on you will be catching people." When they had brought their boats to shore, they left everything and followed him.

LUKE 5:10–11

WHEN JESUS CALLS Simon and Andrew, James and John, they are doing their trade: fishing. Yet they immediately leave their nets and follow him. In Mark's Gospel, it says that James and John even leave their father (Mark 1:20) – an act signaling the sacrifices that the disciples will have to undergo in order to recognize who it is they follow, for the kingdom born in this man, the kingdom of David, requires a transformation that all his disciples must undergo. The new King David is not one whose purple is immediately evident, but rather his power, unlike the devil's offer, can be found only in his crucifixion and following him there. It will take new eyes and ears to see and hear the truth proclaimed by Jesus.

The Gospels are unsparing in their description of the incomprehension of the disciples, but the disciples do follow Jesus. In this respect, they are different from the crowds. Jesus goes throughout Galilee teaching in the synagogues, proclaiming the good news of the kingdom, and curing those afflicted with diseases or demons, as well as epileptics and paralytics (Matt. 4:23–25). Great crowds begin to follow him, even from beyond the Jordan River. They are often in awe of Jesus and express amazement at his teaching. In the end, however, they will shout, "Let him be crucified!" (Matt. 27:22–23). Unlike Jesus, they give in to the devil's temptation.

Even so, early on in the Gospels, we see what is required if we are to be followers rather than admirers of Jesus. The difference between the two is clear. Following Jesus requires repentance, turning away from the familiar to a training called discipleship. There is a change. That change is not a new set of beliefs plus a new set of behaviors. We are not Christians because of what we believe, but because we obey the call of Jesus: "Come, follow me."

A story that theologian James McClendon tells about Clarence Jordan, the founder of Koinonia Farm, an interracial Christian community in Georgia, wonderfully illumines the difference between being a disciple and an admirer of Jesus. It is said that in the early 1950s, Clarence asked his brother, Robert Jordan, who would later be a state senator and a justice of the Georgia Supreme Court, to represent Koinonia Farm legally. Their conversation went something like this:

> "Clarence, I can't do that. You know my political aspirations. Why, if I represented you, I might lose my job, my house, everything I've got."
>
> "*We* might lose everything too, Bob."
>
> "It's different for you."
>
> "Why is it different? I remember, it seems to me, that you and I joined the church the same Sunday, as boys. I expect when we came forward the preacher asked me about the same question he did you. He asked me, 'Do you accept Jesus as your Lord and Savior?' And I said, 'Yes.' What did you say?"
>
> "I follow Jesus, Clarence, up to a point."
>
> "Could that point by any chance be – the cross?"
>
> "That's right. I follow him to the cross, but not on the cross. I'm not getting myself crucified."
>
> "Then I don't believe you're a disciple. You're an admirer of Jesus, but not a disciple of his. I think you ought to go back to the church you belong to, and tell them you're an admirer, not a disciple."
>
> "Well now, if everyone who felt like I do did that, we wouldn't *have* a church, would we?"

"The question," Clarence said, "is, 'Do you have a church?'"

To become a follower of Jesus is not a matter of a new or changed self-understanding, nor a matter of becoming spiritual or going to church, but rather it is affirming with one's life that Jesus is God's Messiah – the Son of God who is the Lord. It means becoming part of a community that reflects the one we profess, the one who is our high priest and king to whom we give our allegiance. To live such a life is to undergo a fundamental change (2 Cor. 5:16–17), to be transformed so as to walk in the light of the new age inaugurated by Jesus.

This is good news. Jesus, God incarnate, invites us to enter into God's history, a story that both disrupts our world and reveals how God is reconciling the world. The stories of Jesus' life don't just display his life and recall his teaching; they train us to situate our lives in relation to him who is the inbreaking of God's new world.

2

Far from Shore

Peter answered him, "Lord, if it is you, command me to come to you on the water." He said, "Come." So Peter got out of the boat, started walking on the water, and came toward Jesus.

MATTHEW 14:28–29

JESUS DOES NOT want Christians. At least not in the sense of people who simply profess certain beliefs about him. As followers of Jesus, our beliefs cannot be separated from how we live. The temptation to separate Christian "truths" from the lives we live is due to fear of being held accountable and leads to a duplicity that gnaws at our faith. Jesus teaches that it is by our fruits that we, and he, will be known (Matt. 7:15–20). To believe that this man, Jesus, is the Christ, God's anointed king, requires that we become as he is. The truth of the story we find in the Gospels is known only through the kind of lives it produces. "Whoever claims to live in him must walk as Jesus did" (1 John 2:6). Jesus' aim is to re-narrate our lives in accordance with his.

To be a follower of Jesus, therefore, is to live confidently and joyfully in the light of Christ's story. Only in this way, only by being a witness to the one who is the truth, can the truth of Christ be seen for what it is. "He who has seen me," Jesus says, "has seen the Father" (John 14:9). As Jesus obeyed the Father, there is no other foundation for living truthfully than to obey Jesus. Those who hear his words and act on them have lives founded on a foundation capable of weathering any storm.

WHEN JESUS' DISCIPLES see him walking on water they are terrified. People do not walk on water. And so they grasp for any explanation that would return their world to normality – he must be a ghost. Jesus responds to their cry of fear and identifies himself as "I am." This is the "I am" of Psalm 77:19, the "I am" who provides a way through the sea, a path through the mighty waters, leaving footprints unseen. Peter asks Jesus to command him to meet him on the water, and Jesus does so with the single word, "Come." Peter walks toward Jesus but notices the strong wind and begins to sink. He begs Jesus to save him. Peter does not begin to sink and then become frightened; he becomes frightened and then begins to sink. Losing sight of Jesus means that Peter, like all of us, cannot help but become frightened, which means we cannot survive. Jesus, as he has so often done, stretches out his hand and saves him.

Peter is often criticized for being impulsive, for having "little faith," and for doubting, but such criticism should not overlook the fact that he asks Jesus to command him to come to him. Peter recognizes that he cannot walk on water by his own initiative. He has no ability to come to Jesus unless his ability comes from Jesus. Peter's faith is little, but he at least recognizes that faith is obedience. Faith is a matter of following Jesus wherever he happens to be. It is, as Bonhoeffer puts it, a matter of being "dragged out of our relative security into a life of absolute insecurity (that is, in truth, into the absolute security and safety of the fellowship of Jesus)."

We are, of course, sympathetic with Peter because we too doubt. Like Peter, we fix our eyes elsewhere and are frightened. Our focus is on ourselves or on what the world values and not on the one who says, "Come!" Our fears are not governed by our fear of God, because, like Herod and Pilate, we fear the opinions of others more than we fear God. As a result, we sink beneath the weight of our natural human desires, hoping others will still think us good, or at least normal. But followers of Jesus, those who refuse to live in a world devoid of miracles, cannot be normal.

Jesus will eventually choose Peter and declare that "on this rock" the church will be built (Matt. 16:18). The church is the ark of the kingdom, but often the church finds herself far from shore and threatened by strong winds and waves. Those in the boat, not to mention those safely on shore, often fail to understand that they are meant to be far from shore and that to be threatened by a storm is not unusual when it comes to following Jesus. If those who profess to be Christian are faithful, they will always be far from the shore. Some, moreover, will even be commanded to leave the safety of the boat to walk on water – a simple matter of responding to Jesus' call.

3

The Kingdom in Person

Now after John was arrested, Jesus came to Galilee proclaiming the good news of God and saying, "The time is fulfilled, and the kingdom of God has come near; repent, and believe in the good news."

MARK 1:14–15

JESUS CAME proclaiming the good news of the kingdom. The significance of the kingdom of God in Jesus' preaching and ministry has become commonplace and welcomed. The notion of the kingdom sounds like it involves guidelines and ideals such as love, justice, peace, and righteousness that can inform a Christian social ethic. But this approach is doomed from the start because it fails to do justice to the centrality of who Jesus is and what he did. The kingdom cannot be made into an ethical ideal, because scripture refuses to separate the kingdom from the one who is the proclaimer of the kingdom. In the words of Karl Barth, "Jesus is himself the established kingdom of God." Or in Origen's classical phrase, Jesus is the *autobasileia* – the kingdom in person.

In the New Testament the proclamation of the kingdom of God and the acknowledgment of the lordship of Christ come together. Jesus' identity is revealed through his relation to God and the authority that relationship gives him to proclaim the kingdom. Jesus' authority and his identity are inseparable from each other. Put differently, Jesus refused to accept the role of Messiah as if it constituted a part that he was playing. Rather, his whole self is an act of participation in God's purpose for humankind. Jesus represents, embodies, and is the supreme agent of the kingdom.

This means there is no way to know what God's kingdom is like except by learning the story of this man, Jesus. For his story defines how God rules and how such a rule creates a corresponding "world" and society. There is no way to talk about a Christian moral framework except as it is determined by the form of Jesus' life. *He* demonstrates the kingdom. *He* is God's parable of what God's kingly rule looks like. Jesus thus invites us to look through him to find the kingdom here on earth. It is not possible to bear witness to the kingdom without responding to him.

The reality of God's kingdom is manifest through Jesus' healings and exorcisms, where he comes face to face with the demons that rule our lives and this world and decisively defeats them (Luke 11:20). It is also revealed in Jesus' relations with others. He enjoys meals with the poor and the outcast, demonstrating a new social order based not on status but on a justice that makes right all our relationships. Finally, God's kingdom is manifested in the calling of Jesus' first disciples, who leave all that they have and make a radical break with security and possessions, with the customs and habits of everyday life, for no other purpose than to share in his ministry of preaching the repentance needed to become part of the kingdom (Mark 3:13; Matt. 10:5–42).

The way of the kingdom, as manifest in Jesus, is quite simply extended training in being dispossessed, of becoming liberated by God from all that we think gives us power over our own lives and the lives of others. And this includes our possessions, which are the very source of so much discontent and violence. Fearing that others desire what we have, we are held captive to self-deceptive justifications that mire us in patterns of injustice that can be sustained only through coercion. But Jesus offers a radical alternative. He offers us a journey, an adventure, in which we are free to embody his peace here and now. Once undertaken, we discover that what we once held valuable, even our very "selves," and what once bound us, mammon and the things of this world, no longer count as anything. We discover our true nature, our true end.

4

Becoming Part of Christ's Story

Jesus went on with his disciples to the villages of Caesarea Philippi, and on the way he asked his disciples, "Who do people say that I am?" And they answered him, "John the Baptist; and others, Elijah; and still others, one of the prophets." He asked them, "But who do you say that I am?" Peter answered him, "You are the Messiah." And he sternly ordered them not to tell anyone about him.

MARK 8:27–30

TO BE A DISCIPLE of Jesus requires a training beyond what any of his first followers imagined. This is the lesson Peter had yet to learn. "Who do people say that I am?" Peter at first seems to answer rightly: you are the Messiah we have long awaited, the one who will restore us to power and glory, who will provide the power to return Israel to her preeminence among the nations. Peter has indeed learned Jesus' name.

Becoming Part of Christ's Story

But Jesus then begins to tell his disciples that he is not going to be recognized as having such power; indeed, he will be rejected and killed. And Peter, still imbued with the old order, the old way of "success," suggests this is no way for a savior to talk; saviors are people with power to effect change in the world. To save means to take control, or to attempt to, and Jesus does neither. His power is of a different kind, and the powers of this world will necessarily put him to death because they recognize, better than Peter, what a threat to power looks like. For here is one who invites us to participate in the kingdom of God's love, a kingdom that releases the power of self-sacrifice, giving, and service. The powers of this world cannot comprehend such a kingdom. They oppose it.

Jesus thus rebukes Peter, who had learned Jesus' name but not his person or the story that determines the meaning of the name. Jesus' word to Peter is not a word for the few. No, if any of us are to follow him, as he called Peter to do, we must learn to suffer and lose our lives for "his sake." We can understand, perhaps, how we might need to lose our lives for family, homeland, or some noble cause – but Jesus says we must lose our lives for his sake and for the gospel (Mark 8:35). It's not as if self-sacrifice is a good in itself. Just as truth is not freeing unless it is *his* truth, sacrifice will not help us unless it is the sacrifice that is done in the name and form of the kingdom as we find it displayed in Jesus' life. There is no truth beyond him: his story is the truth of the kingdom. And that truth turns out to be the cross.

Jesus' death isn't just any death. It is of decisive significance because it was the end and fulfillment of his life. In his death he finished the work that it was his mission to perform. In this sense the cross is not a detour or a roadblock on the way to the kingdom, it is the kingdom come (Luke 9:23–25).

And it is such because the cross, more than any other event, reveals the character of Jesus' mission. Jesus was the bearer of a new possibility of human and social relationships. He reveals God's politics, how God reconciles people to himself and one another. In this way, Christian discipleship creates a new order in which a new humanity is born (Eph. 2:11–22). Being a Christian is an expression of our obedience to Christ within a community based on Jesus' messiahship. It was this that Peter had not learned; he assumed that this kingdom would look like the kingdoms of this world. But he was wrong: the kingdoms of the world derive their being from our fear of, and our power over, one another; the reign of God means that a community can exist where trust rules, trust made possible by the knowledge that our existence is bounded by the truth. Like Peter, few of us are ready for such knowledge, but insofar as we are able to make it part of our lives, we in fact become citizens of his kingdom.

Becoming Part of Christ's Story

To follow Jesus and enter God's kingdom is thus to be part of a new social order, which is formed on Jesus' obedience to the cross. The constitutions of this new order are the Gospels. And these are not just depictions of a "religious" man; they are manuals for the training necessary to be part of the new community centered on Jesus. To be a follower of Jesus it is not enough to know the basic facts of his life and believe them to be true. It is not enough to know his story and affirm it. Rather, to be a disciple of Jesus means that our lives must literally be taken up into the drama of God's redemption of this creation.

To follow Jesus is to adopt his story as our own, a story that teaches us how God's rule in this world is constituted. In Jesus we meet one who has the authority and power to forgive our fevered search for security and significance through greed, deception, coercion, and violence. To learn to follow Jesus means learning to accept such forgiveness, and it is no easy thing to accept, as acceptance requires recognition of our sin as well as vulnerability. But by learning to be forgiven we are enabled to view other lives not as threats but as gifts. Thus, in contrast to all societies built on shared resentments and fears, Jesus calls us to join a community that is formed by a story that enables its members to trust the otherness of the other as the very sign of the forgiving character of God's kingdom.

5

Love Is Not Enough

We know love by this, that he laid down his life for us – and we ought to lay down our lives for the brothers and sisters.

1 JOHN 3:16

LOVE HAS A PROMINENT PLACE in Jesus' teaching and preaching. But Jesus does not urge love as though it were an end in itself, as though it were intuitively obvious or could be embodied as a general principle or policy, for the love that he commands consists in loving others as God has loved us (1 John 4:9). The command to love cannot be separated from the one who commands and embodies it. "I give you a new commandment, that you love one another. Just as I have loved you, you also should love one another" (John 13:34). Jesus does not come to us as a preacher of love, but as the one by whom we might know the righteousness of God's kingdom. He comes to establish the condition that makes love for one another possible in the world.

Love Is Not Enough

The gospel is about this man, Jesus the Christ. It is not about love or some love ethic, but a call of adherence to this man, God's very Son, who has bound our destiny to his, who has made the story of our life his story. To make the gospel into an ethic of love is to leave it at our disposal, in which we fill in the context of love by our wishes. But Christ's story forms us into the kind of people in whom God's love can take shape; it transforms us so that we can become capable of love.

The great commandment, to love the Lord with all our heart, soul, mind, and strength, and our neighbor as ourselves, is followed by the story of the Good Samaritan (Luke 10:25–37). And there is good reason. The oft-cited command, "Love your neighbor as yourself" is not self-evident nor the moral upshot of that story. The story itself is the meaning of love. And that meaning both subverts and transcends our human notions of love.

If Christ was but a preacher of love, one wonders how he could have ever ended up on the cross – for who is going to object to that kind of preaching? He is nailed to a cross because his love comes as the revelation of God's righteousness, which brings pain and change and calls us to extend the hand to those we cannot seem to love. Love is not an easy thing. Our ability to love, not just our understanding of what it means, is dependent on the hard business of following this man and on what he has done for us on the cross.

Jesus Changes Everything

If we are to learn to love as Christ loved, we must first learn to follow him all the way to the cross. We must, as when Jesus washed Peter's feet (John 13:1–10), be wiped clean of all lesser loves. Jesus' way requires humility, forgiveness, discipline, and training. Otherwise, we end up trivializing love as well as our own lives, and the cross amounts to little more than a symbol of our little sacrifices that we associate with doing good to others. In reality, God's love liberates us from what we deem our "better" selves. Christian love faces honestly the conditions under which we find it so difficult to love. To love as Christ loved we must see the world and our own lives as they are. Love cannot be blind – it is a form of seeing. The illusions we have of ourselves and of one another are exposed in our human attempts to love. That is why we are often more honest with total strangers than with those closest to us; with strangers we have nothing to lose by betraying the truth about ourselves.

There is much talk of the church being welcoming and affirming, of accepting people as they are. I don't want God to accept me the way I am. I want God to transform me, to make me perfect. I am going to need a lot of transformation for that to happen. Our lives cannot remain the same when all our desires and loyalties are directed to the way in which Jesus loved. The gospel is not "you are accepted." That's not love. That message is but a way of escaping the necessity of

Love Is Not Enough

judgment on ourselves, ensuring we will have shallow souls. I'm not content with accepting anyone just the way they are. As others have observed, about the worst advice you can give anyone is to be themselves.

Real love acknowledges the estranged condition in which we find ourselves, and our need for repentance and forgiveness. A so-called ethic of love that everyone can readily fulfill fails to address this fact. It is a cover for a kind of relativism, an ethical minimalism that rests on the inherent right to choose and assumes that since we cannot know what is ultimately good, perhaps the best thing we can do is be open and nice to others.

This kind of love is but the ethics of tolerance, an ethic of cowardly kindness and benign affirmation that rests on our own arbitrary desires and preferences. What becomes important is that we are sincere rather than right and wrong. It is no longer possible to think of people doing wrong. It is no longer possible to stray from God's will. It is no longer possible to be evil. We can only be people who are in need and are psychologically sick or broken. There are no longer grave sins that are a result of evil intentions and wrong choices, just disordered loves.

Left with this kind of love, what are we to do, for example, with those who believe that the most loving thing is to stop reproducing for the good of the planet? Or that we should abort all babies with Down syndrome out of love for them, whom we deem unable to live worthy lives? On what basis are we to determine who gets life-saving procedures? Should we employ criteria of social worth to select who lives and who dies, or should we simply leave it to chance? Can love alone decide?

These issues make clear the insufficiency of always trying to do the most loving thing. We are not the most loving people. Besides, the most loving thing can quickly become an ideology of our own self-interest, our own happiness, our own unwillingness to suffer, and our own unwillingness to submit ourselves to the will of God. The task of following Jesus is to face reality as it is; we will fail to do this if we assume that love can come without discipline and suffering. We will fail to do this if we are under the illusion that human flourishing can occur without suffering. It is the worst kind of immorality, the worst kind of unkindness, to rob others of their right to suffer in order to relieve our nagging fear that perhaps we also should be prepared to suffer.

Love is not the saving of others from suffering, but the willingness to continue to love them in their suffering, and patiently hold the pain and guilt that such love cannot help but bring. If we are willing to do that, we might begin to understand why it is that Christ didn't come bringing a message of love but brought himself to die and be raised, that the world and we might live free from the fear of reality.

PART II

Good News

Lord Jesus, humble us so that we will be capable of hearing and obeying your word. We thank you for the gift of yourself in scripture. We rejoice in its complexity and its simplicity. Give us the simplicity to be confounded by your word.

6

God's Possible Impossibility

But seek first the kingdom of God and his righteousness, and all these things will be given to you as well.

MATTHEW 6:33

THE SERMON ON THE MOUNT is an eschatological manifesto. It is concerned with the end of things – the final direction toward which God is moving the world and the reality of God's future in our midst now. This is why it should be read in the light of the kingdom of God. Jesus' teaching, miracles, and healings indicate not only the nature but also the presence of God's coming kingdom. His person and his works are indistinguishable. The Sermon on the Mount is preceded by an announcement of something that God has done to change the history of the world (Matt. 4:23–25). Jesus doesn't teach a new law or depict some impossible ideal. He describes what life is like when God's kingdom breaks into our midst. In the Sermon on the Mount we see the end of history embodied in Jesus, an ending made most explicit and visible in his crucifixion and resurrection.

Followers of Jesus, therefore, are not concerned with anxious, self-serving questions about what we are able to do or what we ought to do to make history come out right. In Christ, God has already made history come out right. The Sermon on the Mount presumes the inauguration of a world in which God in Christ has taken matters in hand. And essential to the way that God has taken matters in hand is an invitation to become citizens of a new kingdom, a messianic community where the world God is creating takes visible, practical form.

This is good news! The Sermon on the Mount is God's possible impossibility, because we are now empowered to live in a world fashioned in accordance with God's peace. "Good news!" Jesus exclaims. "Life is more than acquiring wealth, more than good fortune, good food, more than getting even and getting your way." "Good news!" Jesus proclaims. "There is more to life than satisfying your lust, your greed, your anger, your right to lash back, more than maintaining your image and impressing others. There is much, much more to life."

The most interesting question about the Sermon on the Mount is not, "Is this really a practical way to live in the world?" but rather, "Is this really the way the world

God's Possible Impossibility

is?" What is "practical" or "realistic" is related to what is real. If the world is a society in which only the strong, the independent, the detached, the liberated, and the successful are blessed, then we act accordingly. However, if the world is really a place where God blesses the poor, the hungry, and the persecuted for righteousness' sake, then we must act in accordance with that reality or else appear bafflingly out of step with the way things are. Is the world a place where we must constantly guard against our death, anxiously building hedges against that sad but inevitable reality? Or is it a place where our death is viewed and reviewed under the reality of the cross of Christ?

If Jesus is not the inbreaking of God's future, we are left with only a baffling array of strange commands, which seem utterly impractical and ominous. We ignore the commands on divorce and lash out at people for not loving their enemies. The teachings of Jesus appear to be either utterly impractical or utterly burdensome unless they are set within the proper context – an eschatological, messianic community, which knows something the world does not and structures its life accordingly.

Our hope is to try to live the Sermon on the Mount because this is the nature of our God and it is our destiny that we should be such people. The church is the vessel that carries us there.

7

Kingdom Promises

Looking at his disciples, he said: "Blessed are you who are poor.... But woe to you who are rich."

LUKE 6:20–26

IMAGINE A SERMON that begins: "Blessed are you who are poor. Blessed are you who are hungry. Blessed are you who are unemployed. Blessed are those going through marital separation. Blessed are those who are terminally ill."

The congregation does a double-take. What is this? In the kingdom of the world, if you are unemployed, people treat you as if you have some sort of social disease. In the world's kingdom, terminally ill people become an embarrassment to our health care system, people to be put away, out of sight. How can they be blessed?

The preacher responds, "I'm sorry. I should have been clearer. I am not talking about the way of the world's kingdom. I am talking about God's kingdom here on earth. In God's kingdom, the poor are royalty, the sick are blessed. I was trying to get you to see something other than that to which you have become accustomed."

The Sermon on the Mount rests on the assumption that if the preacher can first enable us to see whom God blesses, we shall be well on the road to blessedness ourselves. The Beatitudes are not a strategy for achieving a better society; they are a picture, a vision of the inbreaking of a new society. They are indicatives, promises, instances, imaginative examples of life in the kingdom of God.

We miss all this when we reduce the Beatitudes to maxims of positive thinking or new rules for getting by well. How many moralistic sermons have been preached urging people to be peacemakers, or meek, or feeders of the poor? The indicatives become imperatives, new rules that lead to conventional forms of ethical activism, anguish, or security, depending on the particular species of self-deception at work in the practitioner. So, being peacemakers "makes sense," for everyone knows that if we do not negotiate a treaty with the Russians, they may blow us to bits. It makes sense to make up with someone, because this will make your life and relationships more pleasant.

We are forever getting confused into thinking that scripture is mainly about what *we* are supposed to do rather than a picture of who God *is* in the world. The basic message of the Sermon on the Mount is not about what works but rather about the way God is. Cheek-turning is not advocated as what works, but taught because this is the way God is – God is kind to the ungrateful and the selfish. Jesus is the Sermon on the Mount. His teaching is not a stratagem for getting what we want; it is a picture of life that is available now that we have seen what God wants and what he does in Christ. We seek reconciliation with our neighbor not because we will feel so much better afterward, but because reconciliation is what God is doing in the world in Christ.

TOO OFTEN the Beatitudes are turned into ideals we must strive to attain. But Jesus does not tell us that we should try to be poor in spirit, or meek, or peacemakers. He simply says that many who are called into his kingdom will find themselves so constituted.

We cannot *try* to be meek or gentle in order to become a disciple of this gentle Jesus. It is by learning to be his disciple that some of us will discover that we have been gentled. Jesus' gentleness is nowhere more apparent than in his submission to the cross and, even there, in his wish that no harm would come to his persecutors. But it is no less apparent in his willingness to be touched by the sick and troubled, to be with the social outcasts and the powerless, and, in his time of agony, to share a meal with his disciples that has now become the feast of the new age.

Part of the difficulty with the Beatitudes is that they seem abhorrent to us – in particular, we do not honor, or like to be, the meek. To be meek is, we think, to lack ambition and drive. You can't be meek and survive the rough and tumble of the world. And that may be so, if the rough and tumble of the world is all there is. Granted, to be meek or peace-loving in a world that knows nothing but mechanisms of getting ahead at the expense of others will more than likely not lead to getting ahead in life. It is no wonder that Jesus' first followers lived in renunciation and want. They are, as Bonhoeffer notes in *The Cost of Discipleship*, "the poorest of the poor, the most tempted of the tempted, the hungriest of the hungry. They have only him. Yes, and with him they have nothing in the world, nothing at all, but everything, everything with God." And yet Jesus saw and felt their suffering and had compassion on them. It is these Jesus calls blessed, not because they are somehow unfortunate but because they have responded to his call that leads to true life.

The apostle Paul speaks of how the foolish things of the world shame the wise, and how God chose the weak things of this world to shame the strong (1 Cor. 1:27). So, look around you. Expect to see those who are the poor in spirit, those who mourn, the meek, those who hunger and thirst for righteousness, the merciful, the pure in heart, peacemakers, and the persecuted. Do not be surprised that you who are called to serve in his cross-shaped kingdom will find among yourselves those who have learned to do justice, love kindness, and walk humbly with God (Mic. 6:8). You will need these gifts, as "unimpressive" as they are, if you are to be for the world an alternative to the world's wisdom. Only a community shaped by such a people – a people who have learned to rely on God and one another for everything – stands a chance of being Jesus' cross-shaped wisdom for the world. It is these he calls blessed.

8

Be Perfect

Be perfect, therefore, as your heavenly Father is perfect.

MATTHEW 5:48

JESUS' MESSAGE in the Sermon on the Mount is good news because it strikes hard against what the world already knows, what the world defines as good behavior, what makes sense to everybody. The Sermon, by its announcement and its demands, makes necessary the formation of a new kind of community, a colony of the kingdom, not because disciples are those who strive to be different, but because the Sermon, if believed and lived, makes us different. In God's economy, it is the world that is alien, an odd place where what makes sense to everybody else is revealed to be opposed to what God is doing. Jesus was not crucified for saying or doing what made sense.

People are crucified for following a way that runs counter to the prevailing direction of the culture. If

Jesus had advocated behavior like turning the other cheek when someone strikes you as a useful tactic for bringing out the best in other people, he could be justly accused of ethical, even psychological, naiveté (Matt. 5:39). If he had said that it makes sense to carry a Roman legionnaire's pack because such an act will help to uncover the basic humanity even among the Roman occupation forces, he might justly be accused of being a romantic with not the slightest inkling of how human beings really behave. Yet Jesus makes no such claims. Rather, as the concluding verses of the chapter make explicit, disciples turn the other cheek, go the second mile, avoid promiscuity, and remain faithful to their marriage vows because God is like this. Disciples of Christ are those who journey forth from the conventional to base their lives on the nature of God, to "be perfect, as your heavenly Father is perfect."

Could Jesus really intend for us to follow this way literally? If not, why does he pay so much attention to the nitty-gritty details of everyday life? Jesus appears to be giving very practical, very explicit directions for what to do when someone has done you wrong, when someone attacks you, or when you are married to someone. It is clear that Jesus certainly thought he was giving us practical, everyday guidance on how to live as disciples.

But did Jesus actually intend for us to embody his teaching in the various social structures of life? Loving our personal enemy is one thing, but how realistic is it to apply this love to the complicated social questions of our day, in a society made up of individuals who by nature pursue their own self-interests?

Such reasoning doesn't reckon on the formation of the visible, practical community Jesus had in mind. All Christian ethics are social ethics because followers of Jesus presuppose a social, communal, political starting point – the church (1 Pet. 2:9–10). As disciples of Jesus, all our ethical responses and practices begin here. Through the teaching, support, sacrifice, worship, liturgy, and commitment of the church, utterly ordinary people are enabled to do some rather extraordinary, even heroic, acts, not on the basis of their own gifts or abilities, but rather by having a community capable of sustaining and forming Christian virtue. The church enables us to be better people than we could be if left to our own devices.

For example, I call myself a pacifist in public because I know I am violent by nature. Hopefully by creating expectations in you about me, I am guaranteeing that you will help keep me faithful to what I know is right. In like manner, I want to suggest that the Sermon on the Mount constitutes and is constituted by a community that has learned that to live in the manner described in the Sermon requires learning to trust in others to help one so live. In other words, the object of the Sermon on the Mount is to create dependence; it is to force us to need one another. Without one another, faith dies the death of a thousand qualifications.

This means that the Sermon on the Mount appears absurd to those not formed into that body called church. This is particularly the case in our society, where we are told that to be human means to be independent, to be able to take care of oneself on one's own terms. So, to understand the Sermon on the Mount properly, we must already be a people who are formed by community habits that cannot be expected of those who do not worship Jesus.

Individuals divorced from the community made possible by Christ are incapable of living the life that Jesus proclaims. All the so-called hard sayings of Jesus are designed to remind us that we cannot live his message without depending on the support and trust of others. We are told not to lay up treasure for ourselves, so we must learn to share. We are told not to be anxious, not to try to secure our futures, thus making it necessary to rely on one another for our food, our clothing, and our housing. We are told not to judge, thereby requiring that we live honestly and truthfully and mercifully with one another.

To be capable of living chastely, to marry without recourse to divorce, to live without the necessity of oaths, to refrain from returning evil with evil, to learn

Be Perfect

to love the enemy – all of these are surely impossible for isolated individuals. As individuals we can no more act in these ways than we can force our wills not to be anxious, for the very attempt to will not to be anxious only creates anxiety. Freedom from anxiety is possible only when we are part of a community that is constituted by such a compelling adventure that we forget our fears in the joy of belonging to the new age.

This way of approaching Jesus' teachings is quite different from many of the approaches to the Sermon on the Mount in Christian tradition. Those approaches are generally about helping us see why the Sermon is not meant to be taken literally. For example, some have argued that the demands of the Sermon, particularly those associated with "You have heard . . . but I say to you . . ." are only for the select few – the religious, the celibate, and so on. But there is no indication that Jesus so limited what he was saying. Accepting this limited application results in a two-tiered ethics that defies our understanding that the whole church is called to be holy.

Others claim that the Sermon on the Mount is relevant for all Christians, but that it mustn't be naively applied. In one's personal life, one can turn the other cheek or do good to an enemy. But a Christian judge or soldier is still obligated to punish the wrongdoer.

One common interpretation of the Sermon on the Mount is that Jesus is presenting an impossibly high ideal to drive us to a recognition of our sin. It is meant to drive us to grace. In other words, it is not really meant to tell us what to do, but rather it reminds us that the Christian moral life is about love. This view makes the Christian life so interior that Christians are to do whatever we do from the motive of love. "Love and do what you will." Bad advice if I have ever heard it! It has an even worse effect on Christology. Why would anyone ever have put Jesus to death if it is all just a matter of being loving?

When we approach the Sermon on the Mount primarily with an attitude of "Do we have to take Jesus' words literally?" we lose sight of the fact that this is a sermon preached by Jesus. It makes all the difference who the proclaimer is – namely Jesus. And he does not merely proclaim it; he is the inauguration of the new age. Perfection is not what we strive for, because it has already come into our midst and is taking effect.

The message of the Sermon on the Mount cannot be separated from the messenger. Jesus is the hoped-for Messiah – the king of God's kingdom – and has made it possible through his life, death, and resurrection for us to live in accordance with the life envisioned in the Sermon. The Sermon is but the form of his life, and his life is the prism through which the Sermon is refracted. In short, the Sermon does not appear impossible to a people who fix their eyes on Jesus, the author and perfecter of faith (Heb. 12:1–2).

9

Subversive Righteousness

For I tell you, unless your righteousness exceeds that of the scribes and Pharisees, you will never enter the kingdom of heaven.

MATTHEW 5:20

JESUS SAYS that our righteousness is to surpass that of the Pharisees and the teachers of the law. He repeatedly cites an older command, already tough enough to keep in itself – "You have heard that it was said . . ." – and then radically deepens its significance – "But I tell you . . ." – not to lay some gigantic ethical burden on the backs of potential ethical heroes, but rather to illustrate what is happening in our midst. His commands are not a law from which deductions can be drawn; they are imaginative metaphors, intended to produce a shock within our imaginations so that we come to see our lives in a radically new way. Jesus' demands push us to the limits, not so much in the immediate service of morality, but rather to help us see something so new, so against what we have always heard, that we cannot rely on our older images of what is and what is not.

Jesus criticizes the Pharisees and scribes for hypocrisy (Matt. 15:1–9), for neglecting the weightier matters of the law while emphasizing minutiae, for greed and self-indulgence (23:23–26) – all criticisms made from within Israel's understanding of the purpose of the law. The prophets had made similar criticisms of Israel's failure to observe the law. Yet Jesus' criticism of the Pharisees and scribes extends well beyond the law; he challenges the very politics of the observance of the law. The righteousness of the scribes and Pharisees, their rightful desire to remain holy, was their attempt to be God's faithful people but without their observance of the law being recognized as subversive to those who ruled them.

Yet that is exactly what Jesus will not let those who would be his disciples do or be. Jesus does not seek to morally improve nor violently overthrow Rome, not because he was outnumbered but because his kingdom is a radical alternative, both to the violence of Rome and to those who would overthrow Rome with violence, but also to those who uphold the status quo. The righteousness of Christ's kingdom cannot avoid being subversive, so much so that it will result in his crucifixion. Jesus calls forth a people capable of living in accordance with God's new order in the midst of the existing one.

Subversive Righteousness

What kind of order was Jesus talking about? What kind of social alternative? What kind of subversive community? This was a voluntary society: you could not be a citizen of it simply by being born into it. You could come into it only by repenting and freely pledging allegiance to Jesus as its king. This was a society with no second-generation members.

It was also a society mixed in its composition. It was mixed racially and religiously, with both Jews and Gentiles, fanatical keepers of the law and advocates of liberation from all forms, radical monotheists and others just in the process of disentangling their minds from idolatry. It was mixed economically, with members from among the rich and the poor.

When he called his society together, Jesus gave its members a new way of life to live. He gave them a new way to deal with offenders – by forgiving them. He gave them a new way to deal with violence – by suffering. He gave them a new way to deal with money – by sharing it. He gave them a new way to deal with problems of leadership – by drawing on the gift of every member, even the most humble. He gave them a new way to deal with a corrupt society – by building a new order, not smashing the old. He gave them a new pattern of relationship between man and woman, between parent and child, between master and slave, in which a radical new vision of what it means to be a human person was made concrete. He gave them a new attitude toward the state and toward the "enemy nation."

This vision is at the heart of Jesus' Sermon on the Mount. "You have heard that it was said . . . but I say to you . . ." (Matt. 5:21–48). There is hope. Murder, adultery, divorce, oaths, retaliation, and hatred of one's enemy are forbidden. This is what the law always required and intended. Yet the community that Jesus calls into existence cannot be defined or motivated by the law or by what it should avoid. Christ himself is the greater righteousness, and his righteousness can be realized because through the Spirit the kingdom of God breaks into our midst and transforms our lives.

In Christ we find reconciliation with the Father and with one another. That reconciliation creates a community that enables us to not harbor anger at our brothers and sisters, but rather to seek reconciliation with them in a spirit of forgiveness. Jesus offers us participation in a kingdom that is so demanding that we discover we have better things to do than concentrate on our lust, our "righteous" anger, our ways of compromising the truth. We discover better ways of being than to break promises or hide behind lies "just to get along" with one another. We need not retaliate against those who would seek to do us harm, thus perpetuating the cycle of violence. We can even show them deeds of love. We can even realize God's kingdom and his righteousness.

PART III

God's Alternative Society

All praise to you, Father of our Lord Jesus Christ, who breathes your church into being, making us members one of another. It is a great mystery that we are your body. But we praise you for it, for otherwise we would be so alone – condemned to live alone, to die alone. But you have given us one another in all shapes and sizes. We do not fit together all that well, but we pray that the puzzles of our lives may please you and entertain you, so that in the end we add up to be your kingdom. Help us to live with the confidence of that kingdom, in the light of your Son's resurrection, so that when all is said and done, this may be said: "They are a strange lot, but look how they love one another."

10

God's New Language

When the day of Pentecost had come, they were all together in one place. And suddenly from heaven there came a sound like the rush of a violent wind, and it filled the entire house where they were sitting. Divided tongues, as of fire, appeared among them, and a tongue rested on each of them. All of them were filled with the Holy Spirit and began to speak in other languages, as the Spirit gave them ability.

ACTS 2:1-4

THE KINGDOM Jesus inaugurated advances through the outpouring of the Spirit. The life, death, and resurrection of Christ was not the completion of God's promise to Israel. Thus, after his death Jesus told his followers to wait in Jerusalem so that the promise would become fully realized. Pentecost is the climax of the Christian year, as only with it can we tell the whole story of God's redemption.

Jesus Changes Everything

But Pentecost is also the beginning. Christ is the living Lord. He is not absent in some far-off spiritual realm. A new era has begun, a new creation is born. All is finally summed up through God's new creation of the church. The mighty wind that gave birth to the church at Pentecost, however, involves the affairs of nations and empires. That wind, that Spirit, created a new nation that was no longer subject to the constraints of the past and the boundaries that keep us apart. God's salvation is the creation of a new society that invites each person to become part of a new age that the nations of this world cannot provide.

At Pentecost God undid what was done at Babel. In Genesis 11 we are told that originally the whole earth had one language, that there was unusual cooperativeness as people migrated together seeking a good place to live. Finding the land of Shinar, they discovered how to make bricks and become builders. Their inventiveness, however, turned wayward. They used their creative gifts to live as if they did not need to acknowledge that their existence depends on gifts. Thus the people said, "Come, let us build ourselves a city, and a tower with its top in the heavens, and let us make a name for ourselves, lest we be scattered abroad on the face of the earth." And God feared that they would now think that nothing they proposed would be impossible.

God's New Language

So God confused their language, and scattered them across the earth into isolated homes, lands, and histories, no longer able to cooperate. This scattering was actually meant as a gift. By being divided, by having to face the otherness created by the separateness of language and place, people were given the resources necessary to recognize their limitations, their status as creatures. God's judgment was the grace necessary to relearn the humility that ennobles.

But our forebears refused to accept this gift and instead used their separateness as a club, hoping to force all peoples to speak their tribe's language. Thus, at Babel war was born, as fear of the other became the overriding passion that motivated each group to force others to become part of their story or face annihilation. The killing begun by Cain was now magnified. Humans would destroy the other even if it meant their own deaths. Our histories, therefore, have become the history of conflict, conquest, and war as we count our days by the battles of the past.

It is only against the background of Babel that we can understand the extraordinary event of Pentecost. The sound that was like the rush of a mighty wind signaled a new creation. The fire of the Holy Spirit burned clean, making possible a new understanding. The Jews of the diaspora heard in their own languages these Galilean followers of Jesus telling of the mighty works of God. God's people themselves, who had been scattered among the tribes, learning their languages, were now reunited in common understanding. The wound of Babel began to be healed among the very people appointed to be a pledge of God's presence.

The joy of that healing surely must have made them ecstatic. It is literally a joy not possible except by God's creation. It is a joy that comes from recognizing that we have been freed from our endless cycles of conflict, injury, and revenge. It is the joy of unity that we experience all too briefly in moments of self-forgetfulness. It is no wonder, therefore, that some onlookers simply attributed this strange behavior to the consumption of potent wine.

The Spirit, to be sure, is a wild and powerful presence that creates a new people where there was no people, but it is a Spirit that the earliest believers knew, and we know. For the work the Spirit does is not different from the work that was done in Jesus of Nazareth, the harbinger of God's rule and reign. In John's Gospel, Jesus tells his disciples that he must go so that the Counselor, the Spirit of truth, might be present to bear witness to him (John 16:5–16). The witness that the Spirit makes to Jesus transforms the witness of the disciples, as they are now able to see what they have seen from the beginning but not really seen at all.

God's New Language

The unity of humankind prefigured at Pentecost is not just any unity but a unity made possible by the apocalyptic work of Jesus of Nazareth. It is a unity that breaks down barriers and draws people together, a unity of renewed understanding, but the kind of understanding not created by some artificial Esperanto that denies the reality of other languages. Attempts to secure community through the creation of a single language, not to mention a single political or technological system, are attempts to make us forget our histories and differences rather than find the unity made possible by the Spirit through which we understand the other as other. At Pentecost God created a new language, but it is an embodied language of care. It is a baptism of fire through which we enter a community whose memory of its Savior creates the miracle of being a people whose very differences contribute to their unity and love for one another.

We call this new creation *church*. She is constituted by word and sacrament, as the story we tell must not only be told but also enacted and embodied. In the telling, we are challenged to be a people capable of hearing and obeying God's good news, a people that in its life together bears witness to God's reconciling work.

To be faithful to God's gift at Pentecost, therefore, the church cannot avoid calling attention to herself.

Jesus Changes Everything

Christ's disciples have a story to tell in which God in Christ is the main character. They cannot tell that story without becoming part of the tale. For God's story in Christ is not just another possible story about the way the world is; it is the story of the world as created and redeemed by God.

That story cannot be told rightly unless it includes the church as God's creation to heal our separateness. For what God did at Pentecost he continues to do; God renews and sustains the presence of the church so that the world might know there is an alternative to Babel. We really do have an alternative to Babel, an alternative to confusion, an alternative to fear of one another, and finally to war. We don't just have an alternative story, but insofar as we are the church, we are the alternative. We are God's new language.

11

Living Truthfully

Speaking the truth in love, we must grow up in every way into him who is the head, into Christ, from whom the whole body, joined and knit together by every ligament with which it is equipped, as each part is working properly, promotes the body's growth in building itself up in love.

EPHESIANS 4:15–16

THE APOSTLE PAUL urges that we speak the "truth in love" in order that we might "grow up in every way into him who is the head, into Christ." Paul notes further that those of us claimed by Christ are freed from greediness and impurity because we have been taught the truth in Christ. So taught, and being renewed in the spirit of our minds, we are to put away falsehood so we can "speak the truth to our neighbors, for we are members of one another" (Eph. 4:23, 25).

These passages help us see why truthfulness is so important for our ability to live together and be at peace with one another. But the desire to speak truthfully, a desire meant to lead us to God and to each other, corrupts our lives when we fail to live the truth we know Christ is. This distance between how we live and what we know to be true is painful and tempts us to give up or to change the truth rather than change our lives. It tempts us to hide from each other because we are not what we appear to be.

We were created to communicate, to speak truthfully to one another, so that we might be "members one of another" (Rom. 12:5). This means we must learn to trust. Trust, like truthfulness, is a gift that is essential to our lives if we are to live joyfully and freely. When the trust that truth makes possible is lost, our lives cannot help but be captured by fear, by forms of duplicity, by patterns of estrangement and disillusionment, and by forms of violence – violence often disguised as order and, for that reason, not recognized for the lie that is at its heart.

That's why any community that isn't truthful is cursed with confusion and conflict. The peace of Christ is not just coexistence. "Sanctify them by the truth; your word is truth," Jesus prays (John 17:17). That word unites us so that we are one as Jesus and the Father are one. Such unity rides on the back of truthful speech, of living truthfully. But truthful speech is more than honesty.

Living Truthfully

Honesty no doubt gestures toward truthfulness, but honesty usually denotes straightforward forms of behavior. You hear people say, "He did the honest thing." Honesty is necessary for our ability to be truthful, but honesty doesn't capture the full reality of being in the truth. To cheat is to fail to be honest, and lying can be thought of as a form of cheating. But to speak truthfully means we sometimes must say what must be said even when we don't necessarily "owe" the truth to the one to whom we speak.

Living truthfully, however, is not just being a straight shooter and "telling it the way it is." This is to confuse candor with truthfulness. The truth will often hurt, but that doesn't mean hurting someone is an indication of having told the truth. The truth sets free because it is meant to be spoken in love.

Being truthful is a skill that requires both character and constant practice and vigilance. We must say what needs to be said in such a manner that it can be received. Regrettably, this requirement can also be used to excuse the failure to tell the truth. What was said at one time and place may have been truthful and good, but at another time and place may not be truthful. Telling the truth is something we learn, and such learning is never in a vacuum, nor is it ever finished, because it is part of our ongoing life with Christ and one another. We must learn to respond to what is going on with one another if we're to understand how we should speak the truth to one another.

All the more, if we are to speak truthfully we will need to commit ourselves to each other; we will need the church to expose the lies that are so prevalent in the world and that would speak through us. This is because our true selves are made from the materials of our communal life. Where is there some "self" that has not been communally created? By cutting back our attachments and commitments, by holding ourselves back from one another, our true selves shrink rather than grow. But to live truthfully means we must be what we seem to be. This is hardly possible apart from being part of a character-forming community. Left to ourselves we become estranged from the gift of each other's lives. Without a community we can't help but lose our way amid the lies that tempt us to live as if God didn't exist and as if we were self-sufficient.

The church is God's gift that provides us with a far richer range of options, commitments, duties, and troubles than we would have on our own. The church is God's school in which character develops and faith, hope, and love are instilled. Without Jesus, Peter might have been a good fisherman, perhaps even a very good one. But he would never have gotten anywhere, would

Living Truthfully

never have learned what a coward he really was, what a confused, then confessing, courageous person he was, even a good preacher when he needed to be. Peter stands out as a true individual, or better, an integrated self, not because he had become "his own person," but because he had become attached to the Messiah and the messianic community, which enabled him to lay hold of his life, to make so much more of his life than if he had been left to his own devices.

If we are to live truthfully, we must be able to confess our sins to one another and, so confessing, experience how our sins are forgiven. To be forgiven and forgiving is what it means to be a community under the cross. It is to walk in the light, free and in fellowship with one another (1 John 1:6–7). Through forgiveness we are freed from our vain attempts to be our own creators, and we discover the truth about ourselves through the one in whom we can find peace.

12

A Community of Charity

There was not a needy person among them, for as many as owned lands or houses sold them and brought the proceeds of what was sold. They laid it at the apostles' feet, and it was distributed to each as any had need.

ACTS 4:34–35

IN LUKE'S GOSPEL, Jesus is almost exclusively concerned with the poor. The poor are blessed (6:20), not just the "poor in spirit," as Matthew has it. Moreover, it is to the poor that the good news comes (4:18; 7:22), not to those of strength or wealth. Indeed, it is exactly the latter who are in deep trouble as their wealth and strength give them the illusion they can be safe in this world (16:19–31). Thus Christ says with no qualification, "None of you can be a disciple of mine without parting with all your possessions" (14:33).

What we see in Christ's concern for the poor and the weak is *how* God chooses to work in history, namely,

A Community of Charity

through the weak. Christ does not make the weak strong as the world knows strength, but rather teaches us how to be weak, as we really are, without regret.

What then makes charity to the weak without regret possible? The crucial question is how to sustain a life of charity in a world of suffering and tragedy, that is, in a world where helping some means others cannot be helped. We are offered in Christ a story that helps us sustain the task of charity in a world where it can never be totally successful. That story is realized in the community of his followers who recognize that when they are weak, God's power is made complete (2 Cor. 12:9).

In Luke's "second gospel," the Acts of the Apostles, we read that to be charitable does not depend on power or effectiveness. Christ's earliest followers were charitable simply because it was the manner of being filled with the Spirit; it was the manner of being most like God (Gal. 5:22–26). Charity is not about removing all injustice in the world but about meeting the need of our neighbors right where we find them. And Christ shows us who our neighbors are. He expects us to bind up the wounds of those right before us.

This is our task: to go and do as the Good Samaritan did. It is through such action that God shows us how to serve one another in a manner befitting his kingdom. This kingdom is not an ideal we actualize "out there" amidst a world that relies on agencies and bureaucracies to get things done. Christians are concerned about the societies in which they exist, but our task is not to make the world apart from Christ into the kingdom of love. Our task is to be a community where charity takes the form of truth. We must first be a people that is shaped by the story that sustains charity in a world where it cannot be sustained.

Though we must, in the interest of charity, ask the state to live up to its own standards of justice, we must never delude ourselves into thinking that the justice of the state is what is required of us as people formed by God's kingdom. It has been the mistake of much recent political philosophy to make justice the fundamental criterion or virtue of social and moral life. Fellowship, community, friendship, loyalty, and truthfulness are equally important marks for any society that strives to be good. Indeed, it may be necessary even to qualify the demands of justice in order to have a society where friendship can flourish as one of its central virtues. In God's kingdom, charity is not an "extra" or an act that somehow goes "beyond" justice. Charity helps us understand what justice actually requires and the forms it should take.

This is why the church is to be a community of charity. "See how they love one another," the pagans said of the earliest Christians. The historical forms of justice

A Community of Charity

in particular societies are often less than the justice that Christians have learned to embody in their life together. It therefore becomes the task of the church to pioneer those practices that wider society, based on law and the coercive apparatus of the state, has not learned as forms of justice. (At times it is also possible that the church can learn more just ways of forming life by looking at society.) The church, therefore, must be a paradigmatic community in the hope of providing some indication of what the world can be but is not.

What might such a community look like? How the economic life of the church is formed, for example, is not irrelevant to how the church affects the societies in which she exists. This not only involves how Christians learn to use their possessions, but also what kinds of professions the community thinks it appropriate for Christians to participate in. The church must again establish that not all professions and roles in a society are open to the Christian's participation. The church must provide the space in society that gives the basis for us to be able to decide to what extent we can involve ourselves in support of our society – in effect, what kind of citizens we should be.

The question of how the church orders her life, therefore, is crucial to what kind of community of charity she is. Does the church, for example, expect and require her leaders to tell her the truth? Politics, understood as the art of the maintenance of a good society, is an art that is at the heart of being Christian. The crucial question is whether we are a determinative enough community that our politics can provide a basis for authority rather than the politics of fear. For if there is no authority that can speak from the shared loyalties of a community, then we have no recourse against those who must resort to power and force, which are often more destructive since they rule by disavowing that they are using coercion.

Finally and most crucially, how Christians care for the stranger is an essential mark of what it means to be the church. It is no accident that Christians were among the first to set up hospitals. These were not a matter of philanthropy. They reflected the Christian social ethic, the kind and form of care the church provides for those who have no other means to defend themselves. The Christian sees the stranger as a neighbor.

As a community of charity, the church has learned to embody the form of truth that is charity as revealed in the person and work of Christ. "Just as you did it to one of the least of these brothers and sisters of mine, you did it to me" (Matt. 25:40). Such charity may be deemed ineffective, but it is the kind of character required of those who are pledged to serve the kingdom of God as Christ has revealed it on the cross.

13

Family and the Church

A crowd was sitting around him, and they said to him, "Your mother and your brothers are outside asking for you." And he replied, "Who are my mother and my brothers?" And looking at those who sat around him, he said, "Here are my mother and my brothers! Whoever does the will of God is my brother and sister and mother."

MARK 3:32–35

THROUGHOUT HIS MINISTRY, Jesus challenged loyalty to family. He did so through the calling of the disciples (Matt. 4:18–22), by his refusal to let the one desiring to be a disciple return to bury his father (Matt. 8:18–22), and through his prediction that in the coming persecutions brother would deny brother, fathers would rise up against their children, and children would put their parents to death (Matt. 10:16–23, 34–39). If there was any doubt that Jesus meant what he said, he also identified his disciples as his true family. His challenge to family loyalty was radical.

Jesus Changes Everything

To be a disciple of Jesus is to be grafted into a new family that Christ has constituted. We are all children of God, but now a community has been established in which we are called to be parents, brothers, and sisters for one another. In such a family there are no "unwanted children."

Taking such a critical attitude toward the biological family could not help but put Jesus in tension with the people of Israel. As a faithful son of Israel, he was expected to marry and have a child, yet he remained single. His singleness, moreover, is a sign that God's kingdom will not grow by biological ascription. Rather, the kingdom of God grows by witness and conversion. Through such growth Christians will discover sisters and brothers we did not know we had.

The idea that the New Testament is "pro-family" is a very difficult position to take in light of this text. Christ brought a new age in which people are not obligated to be married. In fact, singleness is probably the most honored way of life for Christians.

This is why Christian teaching about marriage and sex must be understood in the context of baptism, for baptism constitutes our true family (Gal. 3:26–28). Baptism tells us what marriage means and why Christians marry. Christians do not need to marry, since their true family is the church (Mark 10:28–31).

Family and the Church

It is only against the backdrop of this family that marriage becomes a calling, which must be tested by the community. That two people may be in love is therefore not a sufficient condition for their marriage to be blessed by the church, since the church must be convinced that this marriage will build up Christ's body. Moreover, the Christian understanding of marriage as lifelong monogamous fidelity only makes sense against the backdrop of our baptismal covenant with one another. Any attempt to develop a Christian sexual ethic abstracted from the church's practice of singleness and marriage cannot help but be unintelligible.

LOVE IS THE FRUIT of marriage, the result of our faithful commitment to one another rather than its cause. At the service of marriage, the pastor does not say, "Donna, do you love Don?" Rather the question is, "Donna, *will* you love Don?" Love is here defined as something one decides to do, a future fruit of marriage rather than the cause of marriage, a promise, a vocation of some, but not all. Love is not a feeling, but a commitment, a promise, a gift one makes to God and to another person in gratitude for the gifts given to us by God and others.

More specifically, for Christians, marriage is not for the mutual pleasure or self-fulfillment of the couple.

Marriage is subservient to discipleship. Our marriages are ultimately significant as a means of supporting our ministry, including the ministries of childrearing, conversion of the young, and protection of the old. Marriage is a place where Christians are able to be truthful with one another because marriage is more determinative than their immediate feelings.

Granted, marriage can be pleasurable and joyful, but the pleasure and joy begin not in private concerns but in public commitments and service to others. The pleasure of sex is enhanced by openness to new life and to children. Thus we discover the joy of the primal act of being "fruitful," of participating in the very creativity of God as God intended.

Yes, marriage can become a hellish nightmare of manipulation and violence. Marriage, like nonviolence, is too difficult for a couple to practice alone, too prone to perversion when done outside a judging, forgiving, witnessing, caring community. Some marriages today are miserable not because people are not committed to marriage, but because that is their only commitment. Marriage is symbiotic: it both supports and derives power from our other commitments. When marriage is limited to a relationship between two people, rather than embedded in the practice of the whole church, it tends to collapse under its own weight.

Family and the Church

Marriage alone, the relationship of two detached individuals clinging to one another, isolated from some larger good than their own emotional or economic enhancement, is doomed to fail. For all its virtues, marriage by itself simply cannot lift the luggage. Therefore, in thinking about marriage we first think about the church and our vocation to serve Christ, then move to consideration of how marriage might enhance that vocation. When practiced within the church, marriage liberates us from our own arbitrary desires and gives us something to commit ourselves to beyond ourselves.

GIVEN THE PRACTICE of baptism, parenting is the vocation of everyone in the church, whether they are married or single. Raising children is part of the church's commitment to hospitality of the stranger. Everyone in the church, therefore, has a parental role whether or not they have biological children.

For Christians, children are not solely the responsibility of the parents. Parents are given responsibility for their children insofar as they pledge faithfully to bring up those children, but the community stands behind them.

In particular, the way children with disabilities are received in such a community should be strikingly different from how they are received in the wider society, because the whole burden of care for such children does not fall on the parents; rather, the children are seen as gifts to the whole community. At the very least, the church should be the place where these children and their parents can be themselves without apologizing, without being stared at, without being silently condemned. For this is not just the child of these biological parents, but the child of the whole church, a child whom the church would not choose to be without. Moreover, as this child grows to be an adult, he or she will be cared for as a member of the church.

Such a child may add special burdens to the community, but so does any other child, because every child comes to the community challenging our presuppositions. Some children just challenge us more than others as they reveal the limits of our practices. Christians are people who rejoice when we receive such challenges, for we know them to be the source of our imaginations through which God provides us with the skills to raise children in a dangerous world. The church is made up of people who have been surprised by God and accordingly know that we live through such surprises.

The church is a family of people willing to have their imagination and limitations challenged through the necessities created by children, some of whom may be intellectually limited. In the church, people can have

Family and the Church

children even though the world is crying with injustice. We can do that because we believe this is the way God would rule this world; we do not believe that the world can be made better if such children are left behind.

HUMAN SEXUALITY remains a mystery – the mystery of two persons becoming one flesh (Gen. 2:24). Sexual relations always involve us as whole persons, embodied spirits or spirited bodies, with our capacity to make and keep covenant. Sex tells us about the sort of persons we want to be and to become. We can live our sexual lives as technical experts or as whole (and vulnerable) persons, as pleasure-seekers or covenant makers and covenant keepers, as self-centered individuals or as bearers of new life. Seen biblically, there is in sex a sign of God's intention, for there is an implicit exchange of trust and commitments.

Sex is not just a matter of the depth or intensity of one's affection. It's about the continuity of self-giving. This is why sex is not just about pleasure. There is something deeper involved. We know this, even in our attempts to deny it. Sex is sacred, and we should delight in its mystery. We know this because we know its violation. The sexual act celebrates the mystery of one whole and exclusive relationship covenanted between two persons who are committed not only to each other but to the One who creates and keeps covenant and renews all things – including them. It celebrates a covenant we all yearn for, begun in vows, carried out in fidelity, and given to a future of Christ's righteousness, service to Christ, also and especially service to each other and the children we bring into the world. Such is the delight and sobriety – and adventure – of the mystery of sex.

Fidelity is crucial. Premarital sex may promise excitement and a relationship deeper and more intense than anything one has known before – but only for a moment. Love, however, resides not just in the moment. And this is why sex finds its fulfillment in marriage, and marriage its fulfillment in the church, where self-giving in service to others is learned and practiced.

Christian marriage gives a couple the practice of fidelity over a lifetime in which they can look back upon their marriage and call it love. For in marriage the one we thought would be Mr. or Mrs. Right turns out not to be. That's because we are sinners before we are saints. But the adventure of marriage is learning to love the person to whom you are married. You do not fall in love and then get married. You get married and then learn what real love requires. Love does not create a marriage; marriage teaches us what a costly adventure love is.

PART IV

Kingdom Economics

Thank you, God, for giving us ordinary lives. We love the joy that comes from routine. The time you give us to eat breakfast, to commute, to work, to take care of the children is wonderful. Help us not forget the terror that surrounds us as we dwell within the routine. I eat my bagel while some not far from me starve. I think I would have it otherwise. And in my helplessness, I willfully forget the starving so I can enjoy my bagel. Help us remember. Help us know how to share so that the nourishing routines of your kingdom may be known to all.

14

What about Wealth?

None of you can become my disciple if you do not give up all your possessions.

LUKE 14:33

TO BE RICH and a disciple of Jesus is to have a problem. Christians have often tried to deal with this by arguing that it is not what we possess that is the problem but our attitude toward what we possess. Some recommend, for example, that we learn to possess what we possess as if it were not really ours. This means we must always be ready to give out of our abundance or even to lose all that we have. Christians are told that it is not wealth or power that is the problem; we must just be good stewards of our wealth and power.

However, Jesus is very clear. Wealth is a problem. "You cannot serve both God and mammon" (Matt. 6:24). That capitalism is a system justified by the production of wealth is therefore not necessarily good news for

Christians. Christians have rightly criticized capitalist systems for wrongs done to the poor and to those exploited in the name of producing wealth. But as Alasdair MacIntyre observes in his book *Marxism and Christianity*, the biblical point of view is such that being or becoming rich is an affliction, "an almost insuperable obstacle to entering the kingdom of heaven. Capitalism is bad for those who succeed by its standards as well as for those who fail by them."

MacIntyre's observations are obviously contentious and controversial, but they are right in line with Christ's warning against riches. "How hard it is for the rich to enter the kingdom of God!" (Luke 18:24).

We pray for our daily bread, not our comforts and wishes. In other words, we must learn what it means to live in a community of trust. Such a community teaches us habits that draw us away from the forms of greed given legitimacy by capitalist practices and ideologies that are sustained by each person pursuing his or her self-interest. To be formed in the virtues and by the prayer for our daily bread means that followers of Christ cannot help but appear as a threat to those invested in a system that aims to generate wealth and personal profit. Jesus' disciples do not seek to be subversives; it just turns out that taking Jesus seriously cannot help but challenge the way things are, not to mention how we use our credit cards.

What about Wealth?

THE PARABLE OF THE SOWER (Matt. 13) is about wealth. Interestingly, this parable is not often considered by those concerned with the decline in the church's status and membership in our increasingly secular society. It is hard to imagine, however, any text more relevant to our situation today. Why the church is diminishing and dying, why Christian witness has become so anemic and co-opted, seems very simple. It is hard to be a disciple and be rich. Surely, we may think, it cannot be that simple, but Jesus certainly seems to think it is. The lure of wealth and the cares of this world produced by wealth quite simply darken and choke our imaginations.

Too often those who propose strategies to recover the relevance of the church do so hoping that people can be attracted to Christ without facing the demands of self-sacrifice. For a time, they may be joyful about being saved, but such joy cannot survive persecution, nor can it survive "the deceitfulness of wealth." The shallow character of many strategies for renewal is revealed in the fact that Christians cannot imagine how following Christ might put them in tension with a middle-class way of life. They mistakenly assume that securing a "good life," if not a sign of God's blessing, is at least a legitimate pursuit.

Accordingly, I do not think it a radical suggestion that this parable rightly helps us read the situation of the church in America as Jesus' judgment on that church. Today's church simply is not a soil capable of growing deep roots. It may seem odd that wealth makes it impossible for the word to take root. Wealth, we assume, should create the power to do much good in the world. But wealth stills the imagination because we are not forced, as the first disciples of Jesus were, to be an alternative to the world that only necessity can create. Possessed by our possessions, we desire to act in the world, often on behalf of the poor, without having to lose our possessions.

ACCORDING TO JESUS, it is easier for a camel to go through the eye of a needle than for a rich person to enter the kingdom of God (Matt. 19:24). Our temptation is to think that Jesus' further remark, "with God all things are possible" (v. 26), is intended to let us off the hook. Yet such a response fails to let the full weight of Jesus' observation about wealth have the effect it should. Jesus' reply challenges not only our wealth but our very conception of salvation. To be saved, to be made a member of the church through baptism, means that our lives are no longer our own. We are made vulnerable to one another in a manner such that what is ours can no longer be free of the claims of others. As hard as it may be to believe, Jesus makes clear that salvation entails our being made vulnerable through the loss of our possessions. As followers of him, we are actually meant to depend on each other. My plenty supplies your need, and my need is supplied by your plenty (2 Cor. 8:13–15).

What about Wealth?

A wealth that depends on and ensures our independence from each other is in stark contrast to the new creation.

The story of Ananias and Sapphira in Acts 5 makes clear that Jesus means what he says. Ananias and Sapphira are members of the church. They sell a piece of property, but they keep some of the proceeds for themselves, refusing to tell the church all that they had made from selling their property. When Ananias brings some of the money to the church, Peter challenges him for lying to the church. In response to Peter's accusation, Ananias drops dead, soon to be followed by his wife, who undergoes the same sequence of events. Note well: it is our possessions that encourage us to lie, making impossible the trust necessary to be Jesus' disciples. To be saved, to be part of the body of Christ, is to participate in a people who make truthful speech with one another not only possible but necessary.

IF YOU WANT TO KNOW the Christian commentary on "You shall not steal," read James 5:1–6:

> Come now, you rich people, weep and wail for the miseries that are coming to you. Your riches have rotted, and your clothes are moth-eaten. Your gold and silver have rusted, and their rust will be evidence against you, and it will eat your flesh like fire. You have laid up treasure during the last days. Listen! The wages of the laborers who mowed your fields, which

you kept back by fraud, cry out, and the cries of the harvesters have reached the ears of the Lord of hosts. You have lived on the earth in luxury and in pleasure; you have nourished your hearts in a day of slaughter. You have condemned and murdered the righteous one, who does not resist you.

Of course, our defense is, "We're not really rich. The really rich are those with millions, whereas we just have thousands. We, moreover, give to this or that charity. We do not think of ourselves as deserving such harsh judgment as James pronounces. We're simply trying to get along."

We take no pleasure in pointing out that we fail to tell ourselves the truth about our wealth. There is every reason to want to hide the truth from ourselves. Lying and riches seem to work hand in hand. Indeed, to be wealthy is to be encouraged to hide the truth from ourselves. For example, what is more deceptive than the presumption that I really don't want all that I have, that I'm just trying to prepare a good life for my children?

We are told, "Give to him who begs from you, and do not refuse him who would borrow from you" (Matt. 5:42), and we do not think that could be a policy. But just to the extent that we do not think it always could be enacted in our lives, we become thieves. As Saint John Chrysostom declared, "Not to enable the poor to share in our goods is to steal from them and deprive them of life. The goods we possess are not ours but theirs" (*Homily on Lazarus* 2.5).

We can offer no easy solutions, since we ourselves feel so caught. We know that at the very least we must cease telling ourselves lies about our position. Calvin noted that there is more to being a redeemed rich person than simply not wanting to increase one's gain; rather, it is imperative for us to be poor in our hearts. "Unless we . . . be content with our goods, which God has put in our hands, without abandoning our hearts to them, of necessity we will always be thieves."

Of course, the great trick is to know how to have possessions without "abandoning our hearts to them." We can tell ourselves we are ready to lose all that we have, or at least a good deal of it, but how would we know?

Christians have always thought the development of the virtues of temperance and justice to be crucial for not being possessed by our possessions. Temperance – that is, moderate attachment to the world's goods – and the pursuit of justice – limiting our desires in order to pursue our neighbors' good as well as increasing our desire to render them what is their due – are the ways we learn to be a people who are not guilty of theft. To be able to say "enough is enough" and to see our neighbor's need as a claim upon our possessions are great, though difficult, virtues. Such virtues are necessary if we are not to be possessed by the lust for gain that otherwise seizes our lives.

15

Living on Dishonest Wealth

And I tell you, make friends for yourselves by means of dishonest wealth so that when it is gone they may welcome you into the eternal homes.

LUKE 16:9

THE EARLY CHURCH seems to have known nothing of the distinction between the public and the private, particularly when it came to money matters. We need only recall the story of Ananias and Sapphira to know that money matters are a church matter. Yet Christians today would sooner tell one another what they do in their bedrooms than tell what they earn and what they spend. Which is an indication of what we really care about.

Reading Luke 16 we cannot avoid the question of what it is we really care about – that is, our money and our property. Of course, it is such an odd text that clever people like us find ways to make this parable die the death of a thousand qualifications. Is Jesus really

Living on Dishonest Wealth

commending the dishonest steward? It certainly seems that he is, insofar as we are told, "Make friends for yourselves by means of dishonest wealth so that when it is gone they may welcome you into the eternal homes." What in the world are we to make of that? So we become fascinated by questions about how to interpret the parable in such a way that it might be seen as commending dishonesty and we forget that Jesus is making a claim about our money.

I do not think the realism of Jesus in this parable will let us off the hook. As people who have money, we simply have to acknowledge that it is also dishonest money. We tell ourselves that we have worked hard and deserve what we have gotten. But most of us are privileged in one way or another. We have had the good luck to be born into homes that had the habits that would make us a success. Yet the "luck" of our birth is often based on the fact that our wealth is the result of dishonest appropriation. For example, consider the presumption that the land we currently own is ours. What made it ours? For most Americans, what made it ours is, of course, the killing and displacement of Native Americans so that we could appropriate the land for our purposes.

Which brings us back to the stark realism of this parable. Jesus does not presume that we live in a world where we get to choose between honesty and dishonesty. Rather, we live in a world in which we cannot help but be participants in dishonest habits and unjust systems. Jesus tells us, "No slave can serve two masters" (Matt. 6:24), which seems to presume that we have a choice between being a slave and not being a slave. The truth of the matter is that Jesus presumes that we are in fact enslaved. Moreover, we are never more enslaved than when we think we are masters of our destiny, when we think that we can choose between being honest or dishonest in how we handle our wealth.

Does all this just sound too pessimistic? Surely there is some salvation in this. After all, didn't Jesus bring the good news? Has God really abandoned us to a world of such dishonesty and injustice? Is all we have left a Jeremiah-like response of mourning? "The harvest is past, the summer is ended, and we are not saved" (Jer. 8:20). And if we are not saved, what in the world are we doing trying to heed such a teaching?

I wish I had a good answer to that question. I have no doubt that in the cross and resurrection of Jesus of Nazareth we are a people who have been constituted for God's salvation and God's creation. I believe that such a people are rightly called church. I believe, moreover, that such a people have been given the means to discover, even in our enslavement to the powers that rule the world, ways of being of service to one another. For the church is God's promissory note of the coming of God's justice.

16

Our Daily Bread

Give us today our daily bread.
MATTHEW 6:11

JESUS TEACHES US to pray only for *daily* bread. A more accurate translation of this word "daily" might be *sufficient* or *enough*. To pray for more would tempt us to try to live as if we did not live only by the will and working of a gracious God. When manna was given in the wilderness, the Hebrews were permitted to gather only as much as they needed for each day (Exod. 16:16). Daily we must reach out to God who daily reaches out to us. Daily we wake up to the realization that if we are here, if our lives have significance and substance, it is only because of the daily gifts of God.

This prayer ought to move us toward honest confession. Let's face it. Most of us don't think much about daily bread because, for most of us, at least the people who will read this book, bread is not a problem. Most of us perish from too much bread rather than too little, filling the gnawing emptiness within through ceaseless consumption. We are rich and yet, according to Jesus, rich people are in big trouble.

A woman in a little village in Honduras trudges up the mountain each day to gather and then carry down the mountain the sticks for her cooking fire. She then goes back up the mountain to fetch water for cooking the food. Then she grinds the corn her husband has raised, cherishing every kernel, hoping that this season's corn will last through the winter. The tortillas are made in the palm of her hand. She drops them into the pan, cooks them, and feeds them one by one to her children, the only food they will have that day to fill their aching stomachs. That woman undoubtedly prays, "Give us this day our daily bread" differently from the way we pray it.

For us, we ought to pray for the grace to be able to say, in a culture of overconsumption, "Give us the grace to know when enough is enough," or, "Help us to say no when the world entices us with so much," or, "Forgive us for spending so much on ourselves." In praying this prayer, perhaps we will learn to "get back to basics"; perhaps we will become schooled in desiring what we really need rather than what we desire.

Centuries ago, Gregory of Nyssa noted that the only thing we are permitted to ask for is something so basic as bread. Not herds or silken robes, not a prominent position, monuments, or statues. Only bread. Moreover, we ask, "Give us today *our* daily bread." We are not praying for *my* daily bread; it's our bread, which is shared. Bread is a communal product and a communal possession not meant to be eaten alone. The farmers in Iowa, the bakers in New York, the delivery truck drivers in your town all make bread a corporate endeavor. In this sense, none of us eats or lives alone.

That implies that bread is not only a communal product but also a corporate responsibility. Basil the Great made explicit in a sermon that nothing that belongs to us is ours alone, particularly that which we have in excess of our daily bread. "The bread that is spoiling in your house," he writes, "belongs to the hungry. The shoes that are mildewing under your bed belong to those who have none. The clothes stored away in your trunk belong to those who are naked. The money that depreciates in your treasury belongs to the poor!"

Our bread is not ours – either to possess or hoard. Our bread belongs to our sisters and brothers. Bread is God's gift to everyone, which, like so many other good gifts of God, we pervert by our selfishness. To pray, "Give us today our daily bread," is to radically reexamine ourselves, to acknowledge the claim that God has placed upon us through the gift of bread, to admit the responsibility we have for our neighbor's need, and to heed the call to offer our lives to others.

17

On Judas's Side?

But Judas Iscariot, one of his disciples (the one who was about to betray him), said, "Why was this perfume not sold for three hundred denarii and the money given to the poor?" (He said this not because he cared about the poor but because he was a thief; he kept the common purse and used to steal what was put into it.)

JOHN 12:4–6

IF WE ARE HONEST, most of us identify with Judas. Thief though he was, Judas was right – the costly perfume Mary poured on Jesus' feet and then wiped with her hair should have been sold and the money given to the poor. Yes, if we are honest, we cannot resist the conclusion – Judas is appealing.

Given the world in which we find ourselves – a world that thinks that what Christians believe must make us doubtful allies in the struggle for justice – the Christian concern for the poor can win us some respect.

On Judas's Side?

The cultural despisers of the church at least have to acknowledge that we Christians do some good in spite of our reactionary convictions. So it is good that we burn with a passion for justice. It is good that we burn for victims of a system that keeps them down. The only problem with such a passion is that it can put us on Judas's side.

This means we are profoundly troubled, if not offended, by Jesus' response to Judas: "Leave her alone. She bought the perfume so that she might keep it for the day of my burial. You will always have the poor with you, but you will not always have me" (John 12:7–8). We wish Jesus had not said that. If you needed a text to confirm Marx's contention that Christianity is the opiate of the masses, you need look no further than, "You will always have the poor with you." Yet note: the one who said this was poor. That Mary saw fit to bestow a lavish gift on a poor person, a poor person who was soon to die, is surely to be celebrated – particularly by the poor. One of their own receives a lavish gift. One of their own is celebrated. So, if you are poor, what Mary does is good.

It is true that Christians have used this text to teach the poor to accept their status by suggesting that if they do so they will ultimately receive a greater reward than those well off. The church has also glossed over Jesus' response to Judas by not asking, "What if we did more than cared for the poor?" or, "What if we celebrated with the poor?"

That such questions are not asked reflects a church that has forgotten that Christianity is determinatively the faith of the poor. That is why we who are moderately well off are puzzled by the undeniable reality that the church across time and space has been constituted by the poor. We, the moderately well off, are tempted to think, in response to Mary's gift, "What a waste!" Surely a more utilitarian gift or a more long-term strategic solution would have been more appropriate. But the poor know that this is Jesus, the one who shares their lot, so what could be more appropriate than this lavish gift, bestowed on this man to prepare his body for death?

That is why we must think of the wealth of the church as the wealth of the poor. "The poor you will always have with you" is not a description to legitimate a lack of concern for the poor. Rather, it is a description of a church that has learned that "insofar as you do it to the least of these, you do it unto me" (Matt. 25:40). The church is that reenactment of Mary's lavish gift-giving, pouring out ourselves for the world and therefore Christ.

In the fourth century, the Christian poet Prudentius recounted the life of Saint Lawrence in verse. Lawrence was a deacon in the church of Rome in the middle of the

On Judas's Side?

third century. He was responsible for watching over the treasury of the church. The prefect of Rome had heard that Christian priests offered sacrifices in vessels of gold and silver and commanded Lawrence to place before him the church's wealth. According to Prudentius, Lawrence replied:

> Our church is rich.
> I deny it not.
> Much wealth and gold it has.
> No one in the world has more.

Accordingly, Lawrence promised to bring forth all the "precious possessions of Christ" if the prefect would give him three days to gather the church's wealth. Given the three days, Lawrence used them to gather the sick and the poor. Prudentius continues:

> The people he collects include a man with two eyeless sockets, a cripple with a broken knee, a one-legged man, a person with one leg shorter than the other, and others with grave infirmities. He writes down their names and lines them up at the entrance of the church. Only then does he seek out the prefect to bring him to the church. When the prefect enters the doors of the church, Lawrence points to the ragged company and says, "These are the church's riches; take them." Enraged at being mocked, the prefect

orders that Lawrence be executed slowly by being roasted on a gridiron.

Lawrence exemplifies what it means for the church always to have the poor with us. To have the poor with us, to have Jesus with us, does not mean our task is to make the poor rich. Of course, rich and poor Christians are called to serve one another. Rich and poor alike are called to feed the hungry and clothe the naked. But the church, if she is the church of the poor, must refuse the bargain with death that tempts us to live as if life is a zero-sum game of winners and losers. We are, after all, Mary's people, who have touched and been touched by Jesus. And so we know, like Mary, that through Christ our lives have been opened up to the life of abundance. For Jesus, through his death and resurrection, is that abundance to which there is no end.

PART V

Sowing Seeds of Peace

Ferocious God, we fear your peace. We say we want peace, but we confess that war and violence capture our imagination and our spirits. Violate our violence with the transforming power of your love. Wrench us from all hatreds and loves that are the breeding ground of our violence. We cannot will that your peace come, but through the Spirit you make it possible for us to live in your peace. So fire us with that Spirit, that the world might be flooded with your reconciling kingdom.

18

Habits of Peace

If your brother or sister sins against you, go and point out the fault when the two of you are alone. If you are listened to, you have regained that one. But if you are not listened to, take one or two others along with you, so that every word may be confirmed by the evidence of two or three witnesses. If that person refuses to listen to them, tell it to the church.

MATTHEW 18:15–17

THIS IS SURELY a strange text when it comes to the matter of peacemaking. It seems to be less about peacemaking and more about conflict making. Jesus does not say that if you have a grievance you might think about confronting the one you believe has wronged you. He says you must confront the one you believe has sinned against you. You cannot overlook a fault on the presumption that it is better not to disturb the peace. Rather, you must risk stirring the waters, causing disorder.

On what possible grounds could Christians, people supposedly of peace, be urged actively to confront one another? It seems out of character for Jesus to urge us to do so, and out of character for the Christian community to follow such an admonition. But such confrontation is at the heart of what it means to be a peacemaker.

If you have a grievance against someone in the community, you must go and try to work it out. You must do it first alone, but if reconciliation does not take place then you must "go public," taking witnesses with you. If that still is not sufficient, you must take the matter before the whole church.

But surely this procedure is far too extreme, especially for most of our petty conflicts. I may get angry at someone, but if I wait I discover that I will get over it. Moreover, who wants to appear to be someone who is too easily offended? No one likes people who tend to make mountains out of molehills, especially when they claim to be doing so only because of the "principle involved." More importantly, most of us learn that time heals all wounds, and thus we are better off waiting for some conflicts to die through the passage of time.

Yet Jesus seems to have been working with a completely different set of presuppositions about what is necessary to be a community of peace. It seems that peace is not the absence of conflict. Rather, peacemaking is the quality of life and the practices engendered by a community that knows it lives as a forgiven people. Such a community cannot afford to overlook one another's sins because they have learned that such sins are a threat not only to them but to being a community of peace.

As Christians, we are no longer to regard our lives as our own. We are not permitted to harbor our grievances as "ours." When our brother or sister has sinned against us, such an affront is not just against us but against the whole community. The community cannot afford to let us relish our sense of being wronged without exposing that wrong in the hopes of reconciliation. "See to it that no one fails to obtain the grace of God; that no root of bitterness springs up and causes trouble and through it many become defiled" (Heb. 12:15). We must learn to see wrongs as "personal" because we are part of a community where the "personal" is crucial to the common good.

IT IS AN UNPLEASANT FACT that most of our lives are governed more by our hates and dislikes, more by our rights and standards, than by our loves. I seldom know what I really want, but I know what or whom I deeply dislike and even hate. It may be painful to be wronged, but at least such wrongs give me a history of resentments that, in fact, constitute who I am. How would I know who I am if I did not hold grudges or have my enemies?

It seems our enemies are exactly whom Jesus is calling us to confront. He is telling us that we cannot relish our wrongs. Rather, we are commanded to engage in the difficult task of confronting those we believe have sinned against us. Such confrontation is indeed hard because it makes us as vulnerable as the one we confront. The process of confrontation means that we may well discover that we have been mistaken or have misjudged. Still more troubling, it means that even if we have been wronged, by confronting our brother or sister we will have to envision the possibility that, like the people of Nineveh to whom Jonah preached, he or she may repent and we will therefore have to be reconciled. We will be forced to lose the object of our hatred.

From this perspective, peacemaking is anything but boring. Rather, it is the most demanding of tasks. Interestingly, Jesus assumes that the Christian community will involve conflict and wrongs. The question is not whether such things can be eliminated but how we are to deal with them. Conflicts that involve sin are to be forced into the open. That we are to do so must surely be because the peace that Jesus brings is not rest or denial but rather a wholeness born of the truth.

Surely that is why Jesus is so insistent that those who would follow him cannot simply let sins go unchallenged. When we fail to challenge someone we know who sins, we in fact abandon them to their sin and the consequences that follow. We show how little we care for them by our unwillingness to engage in the hard work of establishing a truthful peace.

We also show how little we grasp what it means to be a community of the forgiven. For here confrontation presumes that forgiveness is also to be offered. How often, Peter asks, can forgiveness be offered – seven times? (Matt. 18:21). We cannot help but be sympathetic with Peter's question, because it just seems to be against good sense to always be ready to offer forgiveness. What kind of community would ever be sustained if forgiveness were always available? But according to Jesus, there is to be no limit to forgiveness. There is no peace and no community without forgiveness.

The forgiveness that makes peacemaking and community possible does not mean that judgment is withheld. The question is not whether we should hold one another accountable but what the basis is for doing so and how it is to be done. To be sinned against or to know we have sinned requires that we have language and correlative habits that make it possible to know what it is to be a sinner. Only on such a basis do we have the capacity to avoid arbitrariness of judgment and self-righteousness.

In other words, we must always come to the other person as one who has been forgiven. Otherwise, we simply exercise power over him or her, as one who as judge is in a superior position. But the whole point of

Jesus' instruction is that we confront one another not as forgivers, not as those who use forgiveness as power or as a weapon, but first and foremost as people who have learned the truth about ourselves – namely, that we are all in need of forgiveness and in fact have been forgiven.

But what about the challenge of making peace with those who are outside the church? First, the church must surely be ready to confront and challenge the false peace of the world, which is too often built more on power than truth. This may well be dangerous to do, because often when sham peace is exposed it threatens to become violent. The church, however, cannot be less truthful with the world than she is with herself. If we are less truthful we have no peace to offer to the world.

And we are certainly not even sufficiently truthful with one another. We fail to acknowledge how some forms of Christianity are idolatrous. When Christianity is identified with national interests or a political party or social ideal, it needs to be called out for what it is. We're afraid to do that because we think people being Christian is better than them not being Christian. But bad Christianity is very bad, and we need to be more upfront about that.

Second, Christians are prohibited from ever despairing of the possibility of peace in the world. As God's creatures, we have all been created for peace. Therefore, we must help the world find the habits of peace whose absence so often makes violence seem like the only alternative. In other words, we must deny the necessity of war. We must work toward attitudes and structures for resolving conflicts nonviolently in the world. There is always hope. "Peacemakers who sow in peace raise a harvest of righteousness" (James 3:18).

Slavery, for example, was once assumed to be part of the natural order. Those who called for slavery's abolition were thought to be foolish utopian dreamers. Granted, slavery still exists, but no one today openly argues in support of slavery. War, too, will continue, but as followers of Christ who live in the light of God's future we refuse to justify war as a given necessity. Why can't this century be for war what the nineteenth was for slavery, the era of its abolition?

We must help the world imagine alternatives to violence that arise from our own habits of resolving differences as the church. Unfortunately, the church has too often failed the world by its failure to witness to the kind of conflict and forgiveness necessary to be a community of peace. Without an example of a peacemaking community, the world has no alternative but to use violence and force as a means to settle disputes. All the more, as Christians we cannot help but rejoice that God has called us to be peacemakers, for what could possibly be a more joyful and exciting task than to be a part of God's peace?

19

No Sword but the Cross

Then Jesus said to him, "Put your sword back into its place, for all who take the sword will die by the sword."

MATTHEW 26:52

CHRISTIANS CARRY no sword but the cross. But this does not mean that we are sent into the world defenseless. In Hebrews we are told that the word of God is sharper than a two-edged sword, piercing the soul and laying bare everything before the eyes of God (Heb. 4:12–13). Scripture is the "weapon" of truth that enables those who follow Jesus to disarm the powers by exposing their lies and deceit (2 Cor. 10:4). Christians are not without defense, having been given God's word to shield us from the delusions that are the source of our violence.

Jesus is clear. Attempts to secure our lives through the means offered by the world are doomed to failure. If we are to find our lives, we must be prepared to lose them. But the life we must be willing to lose is the life lost "for my sake," that is, for Jesus (Matt. 16:25). Self-sacrifice, often justified in the name of family or country, can too easily be tyrannical. The language of such sacrifice is often used by those in power for perverse ends. Jesus does not commend the loss of self as a good in and of itself. He demands that we follow him because he alone has the right to ask for our lives.

Following Jesus is never safe. It's a mistake to justify Christianity as a good way of life because it leads to stability and order. "The family that prays together stays together" – such sentiments cannot help but lead to an idolatry of the family. "Whoever loves father or mother more than me is not worthy of me, and whoever loves son or daughter more than me is not worthy of me" (Matt. 10:37) is a hard saying, but one that makes clear why Jesus must prepare his disciples for persecution. Our fathers and mothers, brothers and sisters, are now found among the disciples and not among so-called blood relations. Let that be preached from the pulpits and see if those preachers will live free of persecution. Not a little is at stake. The violence of nations is often justified in the name of protecting our loved ones and our way of life. Yet it is exactly those loyalties that Jesus calls into question.

Jesus challenges those who would kill in the name of protecting their family and their nation. That he does so, moreover, is a clue for any consideration of the sincerity of Christian convictions. It is often thought that what Christians believe has become hard to believe because of modern science. But the fundamental challenge to the truthfulness of Christian convictions resides in Christian accommodation to loyalties not determined by Jesus.

Jesus will not let his followers kill; but he does demand that they be willing to die. Those committed to nonviolence are often asked, "What would you do if . . .?" with the dots filled in with scenarios that would require us to come to the aid of our spouse or our child whom someone is about to kill. Such situations may actually confront those who follow Jesus, but his claim that we must learn to love him more than we love father, mother, son, or daughter means the answer to "What would you do if . . .?" is not as obvious as is often assumed.

To follow Jesus, to love Jesus, may mean that we and those we love cannot be spared death – a harsh and dreadful love, but a love disciplined by the love of the one who makes life itself possible. To be sure, if the Father is not the Father of Jesus, then to contemplate the death of those we love is immoral. But the Father is the Father of Jesus, and Jesus is the Son of the Father. And this Son never kills, but dies and rises again.

20

A Dangerous Business

If you endure when you do good and suffer for it, this is a commendable thing before God. For to this you have been called, because Christ also suffered for you, leaving you an example, so that you should follow in his steps.

1 PETER 2:20–21

I SUSPECT many of us who are considering identifying as pacifist are, like Augustine, "but not yet" people. There are good reasons for that. A nonviolent way of life at once seems too difficult and too placid. We are not even sure what it would mean to claim to be nonviolent. Who of us is threatened by violence? Besides, some forms of violence seem necessary if anarchy is to be avoided or justice is to be achieved.

Peace, moreover, just sounds so, well, peaceful. To be at peace seems about as interesting as watching weeds grow or, for a Texan like me, watching cricket. Some think nonviolence is a better way to describe what it means to be a pacifist. But the description "nonviolence" has its own problems. The word "nonviolence" is parasitic on violence, for which it is allegedly an alternative. The "not" that makes nonviolence seem committed to a world without violence in fact depends on the continuation of violence. Peace just turns out to be not violence. How useful is that?

If peace is just the absence of violence, it is not clear you will be able to recognize the violence that is inherent in the everyday. Just try standing up for what is right and you will see how violent our world can be. That may seem odd, but it turns out that we may be agents of violence even when we seem to be engaged in everyday interactions. For example, relations between classes, genders, and races often are quite violent even though everyone is "nice."

To declare that one is a pacifist is to be caught in the same problem. Just as it is difficult to say what peace is, it is not easy to know what being a pacifist entails. For many years I have declared that I am a pacifist, but I have never liked being so described. "Pacifist" is such a passive way to say what you take to be true, what you take to be right. Great pacifists – Dorothy Day, Martin Luther King Jr., Mahatma Gandhi – do not seem all that passive. Nor were the first Christians. Yet it is difficult to counter the impression that to be a pacifist is to take up a way of life that depends on others' willingness to use violence to sustain a less violent world.

Indeed, it may be the destructive character of violence that makes it so attractive. If you do not believe that, ask yourself when you last went to see a movie about peace. Conflict, even in war, captures the imagination. "What causes fights and quarrels among you?" writes the apostle James. "Don't they come from your desires that battle within you?" (James 4:1). And what a battle that is!

It is common for soldiers to report after a battle that while they were in the conflict, they were unsure where they were or what they should do. After the battle, a narrative can often be devised that makes what happened seem coherent. Such a narrative, moreover, becomes justification for the war by giving a sense that in spite of the terror of battle what was done had to be done. The narratives become adventure stories that shape our imaginations even if we are committed to nonviolence. It is difficult to imagine a world without war. Did not Jesus himself say that in the last days there will be wars and rumors of war, and that nation will rise against nation (Matt. 24:6–7)? War creates a coherence – distinguishing the good guys and the bad guys – that gives meaning to our lives. It seems there is good reason, perhaps even more persuasive than Augustine's "not yet," for anyone to pray for peace but add the "not yet."

When peace is abstracted from the person and work of Jesus, pacifism not only invites the "but not yet" response but is also rightly criticized for being naive. "Can't we all just get along" turns out to be, as proponents of the use of coercion in the name of justice often contend, a naive sentiment that fails to take the violence of the world seriously.

There are texts in the Gospels that intimate something like nonviolence – forgive your enemies, turn the other cheek – but you will not find in the New Testament any straightforward admonition that commands a strict pacifist position. Some may think that a problem, but it is a reminder that Christians are not committed to being nonviolent as a principle or as an end in itself. For followers of Christ, nonviolence is also not just a strategy. When nonviolence is used as a strategy, as practiced by Gandhi and King, it becomes a form of coercion. Followers of Christ are called to live nonviolently because they live in accordance with a different narrative, and in so doing follow Christ's steps (1 John 2:6).

Too often, I fear, accounts of nonviolence fail to acknowledge that to live nonviolently is a dangerous business. It is anything but boring. Followers of Christ suffer for a reason, for discipleship is quite literally a matter of life and death. That should not be a surprise for those who would follow Jesus' example. "When he was abused, he did not return abuse; when he suffered, he did not threaten, but he entrusted himself to the one who judges justly" (1 Pet. 2:23). Following Jesus' example means being ready to die, not ready to take another's life. Jesus disarmed Peter in the garden. He disarms all who take up the cross.

21

God's Imagination

For he is our peace; in his flesh he has made both into one and has broken down the dividing wall, that is, the hostility between us.... He came and proclaimed peace to you who were far off and peace to those who were near, for through him both of us have access in one Spirit to the Father.

EPHESIANS 2:14, 17–18

THE TRUE HISTORY of the world, the history that determines our destiny, is not carried by the nation-state. In spite of its powerful moral appeal, the history of the nations is the history of godlessness. Only the church has the standing to describe war for what it is, for the world is too broken to know the reality and futility of war. For what is war but the desire to be rid of God, to claim for ourselves the power to determine our meaning and destiny? Our desire to protect ourselves from our enemies, to eliminate our enemies in the name

God's Imagination

of protecting the common history we share with friends, is but the manifestation of our hatred of God.

Christians have been offered the possibility of a different history through participation in a community in which one learns to love the enemy. Through the church we learn that we share the same Creator and destiny. So the world's true history is not that built on war, but that offered by a community that witnesses to God's refusal to give up on his creation. There is only one true history – the history of God's peaceable kingdom. Christians can admit no ultimate dualism between God's history and the world's history. The peace we believe we have been offered in Christ is not just for us but for all, just as we believe our God is the God of all. Thus we do not preclude the possibility that a state could exist for which war is not a possibility. To deny such a possibility would be the ultimate act of unbelief. Who are we to determine the power of God's providential care of the world?

Christians, therefore, offer a "moral equivalent to war," in William James's sense, by first offering themselves in the work for peace (1 Pet. 3:8–16). James rightly saw that the essential problem for the elimination of war lies in our imagination. Under the power of the history created by war we cannot imagine a world without war. But in Christ we can, for God has offered an alternative history through the life, death, and resurrection of Jesus of Nazareth. Such a history is not an unrealizable ideal. No, it is present now in the church, a real alternative able to free our imagination from the capacity of war.

The Christian imagination is not simply a container of images or ideas that we entertain in preference to other images and ideas. Rather, it is a set of habits and relations that can only be carried by a group of people in distinction from the world's habits. For example, nothing is more important for the church's imagination than the meal we share together in the presence of our crucified and resurrected Lord. For it is in that meal, that set of habits and relations, that the world is offered an alternative to the habits of disunity on which war breeds.

In the practice of such a meal we can see that the morality that makes war seem so necessary to our lives is deeply flawed, for it is a morality that sees no alternative to war as the necessary means to sustain our particular loyalties. It leads us to suppose those loyalties can be protected only by eliminating the threat of the other, whether we feel threatened by aggression or merely by strangeness. But in the meal provided by the Lord of history we discover our particularity is not destroyed but enhanced by the coming of the stranger. In the church we find an alternative to war precisely because here we learn to make others' histories part of our own. We are able to do so because God has shown us the way by making us a new people through the life, death, and resurrection of Jesus Christ.

To say the church is the carrier of a history other than the history of war sounds lofty when in fact we know we do not live in such a history. We continue to live in a history determined by nation-states where war shows no signs of abating. All the more, our commitment to nonviolence requires us to live in the world with an enthusiasm that cannot be defeated, for we know that the appeal and power of war are not easily broken. Christians, therefore, cannot avoid attempting, one step at a time, to make the world less bent on war.

We mustn't think of peace as the exception to violence; it's the other way around. With this as our starting point, we can enter into the complex world of deterrence and disarmament strategy believing that a community nurtured on the habits of peace might be able to see new opportunities not otherwise present.

HOW CAN CHRISTIANS go to war against other nations in which they might have to kill Christians? How can we get up from the table of unity and be willing to kill one another in the name of loyalties that are not loyalties to Christ? The sacrifices of war are a counter-liturgy to the sacrifice at the altar made possible by Christ. As Christians, we believe that Christ is the end of sacrifice – that is, any sacrifice that is not determined by the sacrifice of the cross – and therefore we are free of the necessity to secure our existence through sacrificing our lives and others' lives on the world's altars. What could it mean, then, to rise from the table of unity we call Eucharist and kill one another in the name of national loyalties? Is it any wonder the world does not take Christians seriously when we do so – because the world knows in effect we are the world's and not God's?

The deep difficulty with war for the Christian is not just that it is so terrible but that it destroys the unity of the body of Christ. War is the enemy of Christians because war urges us to sacrifice our children to the wrong gods, because it brings people together around the wrong symbols, because it deceives us into thinking that nations, not God, rule the world. War is in incredible moral competition with the gospel of peace.

I used to have a poster on my office door that read: "A Modest Proposal for Peace – Let the Christians of the world agree that they will not kill each other." Some might think that an insufficient gesture, but what could be more radical than Christians' unwillingness to kill other Christians because we understand that as a gathered people we are bound in a deeper unity than that which comes through family, neighborhood, or nation?

PART VI

The Politics of Witness

Holy One of Israel, who called Abraham and Sarah out of Ur, who called us, your church, out of the nations, save us from self-righteousness. You have made us different so that our difference might save the world. But too often our difference tempts us to ridicule because the world, after all, is ridiculous. Never let us forget that we too are the world, and so also ridiculous. Shape the judgments of our neighbors and our own foolish judgments by your love, so that we might be together saved.

22

The First Task of the Church

Beloved, I urge you as aliens and exiles to abstain from the desires of the flesh that wage war against the soul. Conduct yourselves honorably among the gentiles, so that, though they malign you as evildoers, they may see your honorable deeds and glorify God when he comes to judge.

1 PETER 2:11–12

THE SOCIAL THRUST of the gospel, and thus the aim of Christian social ethics, is not primarily an attempt to make the world more peaceable and just. Put starkly, the first task of the church when it comes to social ethics is to be the church. Such a claim may well sound self-serving or irrelevant until we remember that what makes the church the church is its faithful manifestation of the peaceable kingdom in the world. As such, the church does not have a social ethic; the church is a social ethic.

The church is where the stories of Israel and Jesus are told, enacted, and heard, and as a Christian people there is literally nothing more important we can do. But the telling of that story requires that we be a particular kind of people, if we and the world are to hear the story truthfully.

This means that the church must never cease from being a community of peace and truth in a world of mendacity and fear. The church does not let the world set her agenda about what constitutes a viable social ethic; the church sets her own agenda. She does this first by having the patience amid the injustice and violence of this world to care for the widow, the poor, and the orphan. Such care, from the world's perspective, may seem to contribute little to the cause of justice, yet unless we take the time for such care, neither we nor the world can know what God's justice looks like.

The scandal of the disunity of the church is even more painful when we recognize this social task. For we who have been called to be the foretaste of the peaceable kingdom cannot, it seems, maintain peace among ourselves. As a result, we abandon the world to its own devices. And the divisions in the church are not just those based on doctrine, history, or practices, important though these are. No, the deepest and most painful divisions afflicting the church are those based on class, race, and nationality that we have sinfully accepted as written into the nature of things.

The First Task of the Church

Again, the first social task of the church – the people capable of remembering and telling the story of God we find in Jesus – is to be the church and thus help the world understand itself as the world. The world, to be sure, is God's world, God's good creation, which is all the more distorted by sin because it is still bounded by God's goodness. The church, therefore, is not anti-world, but rather an attempt to show what the world is meant to be as God's good creation.

The world needs the church, but not to help it run more smoothly or make it a better and safer place for Christians to live. Rather, the world needs the church because without the church the world does not know what it is nor who God is. The only way for the world to know that it is being redeemed is for the church to point to the Redeemer by being a redeemed people. The way for the world to know that it needs redeeming, that it is broken and fallen, is for the church to enable the world to strike hard against something that is an alternative to what the world offers.

Without such a "contrast model" the world has no way to know and feel the oddness of its dependence on power for survival. Because there exists a community formed by the story of Christ, the world can know what it means to be a society committed to the growth of individual gifts and differences, where the otherness of the other can be welcomed as a gift rather than a threat.

A striking fact about the church is that the story of Jesus provides the basis to break down arbitrary and false barriers between people. This story teaches us to regard the other as a fellow member of God's kingdom. Such regard is not based on facile doctrines of tolerance or equality, but is forged from our common experience of being trained to be disciples of Jesus. The universality of the church is based on the particularity of Jesus' story and on the fact that his story trains us to see one another as God's people. Because we have been so trained, we are able to see and condemn the narrow loyalties that divide us from one another.

Like the early Christians, we must learn that understanding Jesus' life is inseparable from learning how to live our own. That means being the kind of people who can bear the burden of Jesus' story with joy. We, no less than the first Christians, are the continuation of the truth made possible by God's rule. We continue this truth when we see that the struggle of each to be faithful to the gospel is essential to our own lives. I understand my own story through seeing the different ways in which others are called to be his disciples. If we so help one another, perhaps, like the early Christians when challenged about the viability of their faith, we can say, "But see how we love one another."

The First Task of the Church

The church provides the space and time necessary for developing skills of interpretation and discrimination sufficient to help us recognize the possibilities and limits of our society. In developing such skills, the church and Christians must be uninvolved in the politics of society and involved in the polity that is the church. The challenge of Christian social ethics in our secular polity is no different than in any time or place – it is always the Christian social task to form a society that is built on truth rather than fear.

So our response to an issue like abortion is something communal, social, and political, but utterly ecclesial – something like baptism. Whenever a person is baptized, the church adopts that person into a new family. Therefore, we cannot say to the pregnant fifteen-year-old, "Abortion is a sin. It is your problem." Rather, it is our problem. We ask ourselves what sort of church we would need to be to enable an ordinary person like her to be the sort of disciple Jesus calls her to be.

More importantly, her presence in our community offers the church the wonderful opportunity to be the church, to honestly examine our own convictions and see whether or not we are living true to those convictions. She is seen by us not as some pressing social problem to be solved in such a way as to relieve our own responsibility for her and the necessity of our sacrificing on her behalf (for our story teaches us to seek such responsibility and sacrifice, not to avoid it through governmental aid). Rather, we are graciously given the eyes to see her as a gift of God sent to help ordinary people like us to discover the church as the body of Christ.

The most interesting, creative political solutions we Christians have to offer our troubled society are not new laws, advice to policymakers, or increased funding for social programs – although we may support such efforts from time to time. The most creative social strategy we have to offer is to be the church. Here we show the world a manner of life that it can never achieve through social coercion or governmental action. We serve the world by showing it something that it is not, namely, a place where God is forming a family out of strangers.

23

Jesus Is King

Jesus answered, "My kingdom does not belong to this world. If my kingdom belonged to this world, my followers would be fighting to keep me from being handed over to the Jews. But as it is, my kingdom is not from here."

JOHN 18:36

"MY KINGDOM is not from this world." Few verses from the Bible have caused more trouble than this one. We think, for example, that with these words Jesus anticipates the distinction between religion and politics necessary to sustain our assumption that religion and politics do not or should not mix. Some have even argued that Jesus' claim that his kingdom is not of this world makes him the founder of democratic social orders, at least to the extent that such orders depend on the distinction between church and state. If that were so, it would be appropriate to give thanks for America because it is the fruit of Jesus' confrontation with Pilate.

Jesus Changes Everything

I have to tell you, however, that Jesus would find this very problematic, to the extent that America avoids recognizing that Jesus is a king. It is hard for us to understand that we stand with Pilate before Jesus because we think we have little use for any king. After all, does America not end kingship in favor of the rule of the people? Were we Americans not taught from grade school on that the American Revolution was justified because the American people rightly wanted no king to rule them? Kingships, after all, are arbitrary forms of government left behind by enlightened and rational people like us. We are a people who are ruled only by ourselves expressed through our chosen representatives.

That, of course, results in one minor problem: Jesus does not want to be our democratically elected leader. Indeed, he is quite insistent that we do not get to choose him. He gets to elect us. He is, after all, the heir to David's throne. David, moreover, was every inch a king, chosen not by the people but by God. Even though kingship had ended for Israel, there is no question that Jesus reclaimed that role for himself. Only now he is king not only of Israel but also of all creation (Col. 1:15–17).

That Jesus is undeniably a king has, unfortunately, led to thousands of bad sermons trying to explain to a democratic people how to avoid the obvious. Thus, we have been told that what it means for Jesus to be king

Jesus Is King

is that he is the lord of our hearts, or that our ultimate loyalty must finally be to God. The only problem with such claims is that we have no idea how we might know what it means for Jesus to be lord of our hearts or our ultimate loyalty.

If you think that all Jesus meant by claiming kingship is that he wants to rule each individual's heart, then why was he killed? Jesus was killed because, as Pilate himself observed, he was a king – this meant that he was the enemy of the emperor and accordingly should be killed. Pilate did his duty, as he should have as a servant of the emperor. So, Jesus was rightly killed with the inscription written in Hebrew, Latin, and Greek, "The King of the Jews" – a king, accordingly, who reigned over all people.

Caesar always wants it all. It's no good to distinguish between the public and the private, thinking that Caesar rules the public and that God rules in our private lives. Such a distinction turns out to merely hide from us how thoroughly we are ruled by the rulers of this world.

Notice that everything depends on how we understand "world." I fear that too often we read, "My kingdom is not from this world," without reading the next sentence. Jesus says, "If my kingdom belonged to this world, my followers would be fighting to keep me from being handed over to the Jews. But as it is, my kingdom is not from here." Jesus does not disavow his rule. Rather, he says that his kingdom is not one that will triumph through violence, but it is no less a kingdom because of that disavowal.

Jesus is no less political for declaring that his followers do not use the sword in defense of the kingdom of God. Yet, if they do not use the sword, what weapon do they have? What weapon did the first church use to advance the good news of Christ's lordship? "Pilate asked him, 'So you are a king?' Jesus answered, 'You say that I am a king. For this I was born, and for this I came into the world, to testify to the truth. Everyone who belongs to the truth listens to my voice'" (John 18:37). Truth is our weapon. Truth is the only alternative to the politics of the sword.

ALTHOUGH IT IS GOOD that the church is free to worship and preach the gospel, such freedom only matters if the church actually demonstrates God's alternative. Are we a people who make it interesting for a society to acknowledge our freedom? The question is not whether the church has the freedom to preach the gospel, but whether she preaches the gospel as truth and is capable of saying no to the state. No state, particularly the democratic state, is kept in check merely by its constitution. Rather, states are limited by a people with the imagination and courage to challenge the state's inveterate temptation to ask us to compromise our loyalty to God.

Because we assume that democracies protect our freedoms as Christians, we may well miss the ways in which the democratic state remains a state that continues to wear the head of the beast. Democratic societies and states, no less than totalitarian ones, reserve the right to command our conscience to take up arms and kill.

In this respect, democracy has been a particularly subtle temptation for Christianity. Christians have never killed as willingly as when they have been asked to do so for "freedom." One of the most important challenges facing Christians today is to remember that the democratic state is still a state and that in so many ways it asks us to qualify our loyalty to God in the name of some lesser loyalty.

As Christians we seek not to be free but to be faithful disciples of our Lord, who would not employ violence to avoid death at the hands of a state. Just as that oppressive regime could not prevent his authorization of God's kingdom, so neither as Christians do we believe any worldly power can stop us from living true to God's peaceable kingdom. Worldly powers can kill us, but they cannot rob our death, any more than they could rob Jesus' death, of its service to God.

24

Christian Politics

I have given them your word, and the world has hated them because they do not belong to the world, just as I do not belong to the world. I am not asking you to take them out of the world, but I ask you to protect them from the evil one. They do not belong to the world, just as I do not belong to the world. Sanctify them in the truth; your word is truth.

JOHN 17:14–17

CHRISTIAN POLITICS has come to mean social activism. Conservative and liberal Christians may differ on the particulars of just what a truly Christian social agenda looks like, but we are one in our agreement that we should use our democratic power in a responsible way to make the world a better place. There are those who want "born again," "pro-family" people in places of power. Prayers must be said in public schools in order to counter secular humanism. Others urge the government to use military power in a restrained and humane manner to secure our livelihoods while also pressuring lawmakers to level the economic playing field.

Whether in the name of social justice or the sanctity of life, activist Christians want to apply their faith to the public sphere. But in doing so, faith in Christ is rendered unnecessary, since everybody already believes in peace and justice even when not everybody believes in God.

Whenever we try to advance a Christian ethic simply by pressuring the government to pass laws or to spend tax money, we fail to do justice to the radically communal quality of the church. In fact, much of what passes for Christian social concern today is the social concern of a church that seems to have despaired of being the church. Unable through our preaching, baptism, and witness to form a visible community of faith, we content ourselves with ersatz Christian ethical activity – lobbying our representatives to support progressive or conservative strategies, asking the culture at large to be a little less racist, a little less promiscuous, a little less violent. We presume that there is no way for the gospel to be present in our world without asking, and if necessary pressuring, the world to support our convictions through its own social and political institutions. The result is not the furtherance of the gospel but a civil religion.

Jesus Changes Everything

Christians today want to be good capitalists and yet also be concerned about the poor. We think the best way to do both is to learn more about economics in order to make our economic systems more just. As a result, Christian calls for justice assume that the market as we know it is a necessity. With the best will in the world we try to grow the economy in the hope that the poor will receive their allotted share. So justice turns out to be a way we comfort ourselves with the illusion that we can help the poor by subjecting them to the same economic modes of thought and practices that dominate our own lives. We simply cannot envision the possibility that capitalism, and the economic sciences that are meant to make capitalism inevitable, might be the kind of powers, the "elementary spirits," that Paul knew undermined God's kingdom of justice (Col. 2:8).

PEOPLE RIGHTLY COMPLAIN that the political agenda of conservative Christians looks suspiciously like the political agenda of secular conservatives while liberal Christians espouse the same social position as secular liberals. In its effort to be relevant and noticed, to be "in the world," the church becomes "of the world" – the dull exponent of conventional political ideas with a vaguely religious tint. Political theologies, whether of the left or the right, generally maintain the existing social order, wherein the church justifies herself as a helpful, if sometimes complaining, prop for the state. Instead of the church providing an alternative, she presumes that God's vision for advancing his kingdom in the world lies in the powers that be.

Here, Christendom's decline is the church's gain. The loss of Christianity in the public square that many bemoan today actually gives us an opportunity to reclaim the freedom to proclaim and demonstrate the truth of the gospel in a way we cannot when we try to serve the nation as one among many helpful props of the state. As Christians lose status and power in the wider society, that loss can make us free. As a people with nothing to lose anymore, we might as well go ahead and live the way Jesus wants us to. We don't have to be in control or be tempted to use the means of control.

Truth matters. We are to be people of truth. The truth that makes us Christians means we are a people who are not destined to be celebrated in any social order, whether it calls itself democratic or not. Do not misunderstand; I am not suggesting that there are not better and worse forms of social and political organization. But Christians are a people who believe that what we believe is true. Such a people cannot help from time to time coming into conflict with regimes organized on the assumption that there is no truth other than what "the people" say is the truth.

Christianity is unintelligible without enemies (2 Tim. 3:12). Indeed, the whole point of Christianity is to produce the right kind of enemies. We have been beguiled by our established status to forget that to be a Christian is to be made part of an army against armies. When Caesar becomes a member of the church the enemy becomes internalized. Our problem is no longer that the church is seen as a threat to the political order, but that now the battle is within.

Jesus is Lord. "Lord" is not a democratic title; it is a truthful designation for the one we worship and obey. We have the authority to testify to the truth that Jesus is Lord. This is not some general truth that can be known without witnesses. A truth known only to witnesses to Jesus cannot help but be a deep and profound challenge to the status quo, because the status quo is based on the assumption that whatever is true must be available to anyone. Christians are not anyone. We are people who Jesus says will be hated and even put to death. But if Jesus is who he says he is, what choice do we have? After all, we did not elect Jesus. He elected us.

25

The Difference Christ Makes

Let each of you remain in the condition in which you were called. Were you a slave when called? Do not be concerned about it. Even if you can gain your freedom, make the most of it. For whoever was called in the Lord as a slave is a freed person belonging to the Lord, just as whoever was free when called is a slave belonging to Christ. You were bought with a price; do not become slaves of humans. In whatever condition you were called, brothers and sisters, there remain with God.

1 CORINTHIANS 7:20–24

PAUL'S REMARKS about slavery are but one aspect of his general admonition to the Corinthian church that becoming Christian does not entail radically trying to change one's place in life. "Let each of you remain in the condition in which you were called." Not exactly a revolutionary doctrine. Could it be that the critics are right, that Christianity tells the oppressed to be happy with their lot and focus their hopes on the life to come?

Of course, Paul tells those who may be slaves that if a chance for liberty should come they should take it. Moreover, he says that whoever was a slave when they were called is now a free person belonging to the Lord. And whoever was a free person when they were called, Paul says, is now a slave of Christ. Yet that does not sound like good news. Onesimus is still Philemon's slave. Philemon may now be a slave of Christ and Onesimus may now be free in Christ, but what good is such a freedom or slavery if that freedom or slavery has no outward effect? Paul's "rule" that we are to remain as we were seems to spiritualize the gospel in a manner that makes it good news only for those in power. I am not sure what good it does, for example, to tell those who are in power, those who are rich or have social or political status, that they are really slaves of Christ.

For many of us, a Christianity that makes no earthly difference is profoundly offensive. No longer sure that what we believe as Christians is true, we at least want to claim that Christianity represents moral positions that are progressive. We want the church to make a difference. What good is what we do in church Sunday after Sunday if it does not mobilize us to work to end the injustices that continue to grip our lives? Paul's instruction to the Corinthians, "Let each of you remain in the

The Difference Christ Makes

condition in which you were called," does not sound like the difference we want the church to make.

However, this is but a reminder of our distance from Paul. Paul does not think that the church has to make a difference. Rather, for Paul, Christians must learn how to live in the light of the difference Jesus has made. That difference is named quite clearly in Mark's Gospel: "Now after John was arrested, Jesus came to Galilee, proclaiming the good news of God, and saying, 'The time is fulfilled, and the kingdom of God has come near; repent and believe the good news'" (Mark 1:14–15). The world has been turned upside down because God has redeemed time by entering our time. The difference has come and his name is Jesus.

That difference, that name, is one that challenges the thrones and dominions of this world. The powers, moreover, know they are under attack. Otherwise why is John in jail? Why is Paul in jail when he writes to Philemon? Why was Martin Luther King Jr. in jail when he wrote his letter from Birmingham? "Repent, and believe the good news" is the radical proclamation that Jesus has unleashed a movement that puts in jeopardy the powers of this world, powers that gain their power from our fear of death and of one another.

The difference Jesus makes is the difference Paul takes as a given when he tells the Corinthians to remain as they were before they were called. They can remain in the position in which they find themselves, not because nothing has changed, but because everything has changed. Note that Paul reminds the Corinthians, "You were bought with a price; do not become slaves of human masters. In whatever condition you were called, brothers and sisters, there remain with God." "Brothers and sisters"? Paul reminds the Corinthians they are brothers and sisters. They are now members of a new family.

"Brothers and sisters" denotes the new reality made possible by Jesus' announcement that the time is now fulfilled. The name of that new reality is "church." A people have been brought into existence across time and space so that the world may know, through the work of the Holy Spirit, what Jesus has done and how that changes everything. The powers of domination have been defeated, having been exposed at the crucifixion as mere pretenders lacking substance (Col. 2:15). As followers of Jesus, we can remain in the condition in which we find ourselves because we are a people with a new freedom that saves us from those forms of life fueled by pretensions of status and power.

Christians hunger and thirst for righteousness and justice, but we are not utopians. Failing to achieve their ideals, utopians and idealists too easily become cynics who, in their frustration, are willing to kill in the name of a good cause. Christians are revolutionaries, but we believe the revolution has happened and we are it.

It happens secretly, patiently, and without fanfare. It happens regardless of what status the state gives us. And it happens, as Paul says, without force (Philem. 14).

We should be ready to be surprised by what God may do to us and with us. We may have thought we could just show up on Sunday to hear the word of God and share a meal, but before we know it we may find ourselves in jail because we are Christians. Being the church of Jesus Christ could actually get us in trouble, just as John the Baptist and Paul got in trouble. Being the church could be dangerous once again. By God, sisters and brothers, being Christian could turn out to be more interesting than we had imagined.

Sources

The chapters in this book are drawn from Stanley Hauerwas's previously published writings, though he has revised them for this volume. Some chapters tie several essays, sermons, and new strands of thought into one piece. The references below indicate the primary sources for each chapter.

Epigraph: *In Conversation*, 107.

Part I: Following Jesus

Prayer: *Prayers Plainly Spoken*, 27.

1. Come, Follow Me: *Matthew*, 56–57; *The Peaceable Kingdom*, 73–74.
2. Far from Shore: "The Way of the Church" in *Preaching the Sermon on the Mount*, 42–43; *Matthew*, 140–141.
3. The Kingdom in Person: *The Peaceable Kingdom*, 82–86.
4. Becoming Part of Christ's Story: *A Community of Character*, 44–52.
5. Love Is Not Enough: *Vision and Virtue*, 111–126.

Part II: Good News

Prayer: *Prayers Plainly Spoken*, 69.

6. God's Possible Impossibility: *Resident Aliens*, 86–92.
7. Kingdom Promises: *Resident Aliens*, 83–86.
8. Be Perfect: *Unleashing the Scripture*, 64–72; *Resident Aliens*, 74–77, 81–83.
9. Subversive Righteousness: *Matthew*, 66–73.

Part III: God's Alternative Society

Prayer: *Prayers Plainly Spoken*, 102.

10. God's New Language: *Christian Existence Today*, 47–54.
11. Living Truthfully: *A Community of Character*, 145–147; *The Character of Virtue*, 51–58.
12. A Community of Charity: *Truthfulness and Tragedy*, 132–143.

13. Family and the Church: *The Truth About God*, 97–102; *Dispatches from the Front*, 182–183; "From Conduct to Character: A Guide to Sexual Adventure" in *Christian Perspectives on Sexuality and Gender*, 179–181.

Part IV: Kingdom Economics
   Prayer: *Prayers Plainly Spoken*, 89.
14. What about Wealth?: *Matthew*, 80–83, 129–130, 174–175; *The Truth About God*, 112–115.
15. Living on Dishonest Wealth: *Sanctify Them in the Truth*, 249–252.
16. Our Daily Bread: *Lord, Teach Us*, 73–77.
17. On Judas's Side?: *Christianity, Democracy, and the Radical Ordinary*, 106–110; *A Cross-Shattered Church*, 97–98.

Part V: Sowing Seeds of Peace
   Prayer: *Prayers Plainly Spoken*, 80.
18. Habits of Peace: *Christian Existence Today*, 89–97; "Peacemaking Is Political"; *Where Resident Aliens Live*, 42–45; *War and the American Difference*, 42–56.
19. No Sword but the Cross: *Matthew*, 109–110.
20. A Dangerous Business: "Give Us Peace – But Not Yet"; "Peacemaking Is Political."
21. God's Imagination: *Should War be Eliminated?* 53–58.

Part VI: The Politics of Witness
   Prayer: *Prayers Plainly Spoken*, 45.
22. The First Task of the Church: *A Community of Character*, 44–52, 74; *The Peaceable Kingdom*, 99–105; *Resident Aliens*, 81–83.
23. Jesus Is King: *Disrupting Time*, 58–61; *After Christendom*, 70–72; *Against the Nations*, 127–129.
24. Christian Politics: *Resident Aliens*, 37–39, 80–81; *Sanctify Them in the Truth*, 223–224; *Minding the Web*, 262–263; "Peacemaking Is Political."
25. The Difference Christ Makes: *A Cross-Shattered Church*, 99–104.

Bibliography

Berkman, John, and Michael Cartwright, eds. *The Hauerwas Reader*. Duke University Press, 2001.

Fleer, David, and Dave Bland, eds. *Preaching the Sermon on the Mount: The World It Imagines*. Chalice, 2007.

Hauerwas, Stanley. *After Christendom: How the Church Is to Behave If Freedom, Justice, and a Christian Nation Are Bad Ideas*. Abingdon, 1999.

Hauerwas, Stanley. *Against the Nations: War and Survival in a Liberal Society*. Winston, 1985.

Hauerwas, Stanley. *The Character of Virtue: Letters to a Godson*. Eerdmans, 2018.

Hauerwas, Stanley. *Christian Existence Today: Essays on Church, World, and Living In Between*. Labyrinth, 1988.

Hauerwas, Stanley. *A Community of Character: Toward a Constructive Christian Social Ethic*. University of Notre Dame Press, 1981.

Hauerwas, Stanley. *A Cross-Shattered Church: Reclaiming the Theological Heart of Preaching*. Brazos, 2009.

Hauerwas, Stanley. *Dispatches from the Front: Theological Engagements with the Secular*. Duke University Press, 1994.

Hauerwas, Stanley. *Disrupting Time: Sermons, Prayers, and Sundries*. Cascade, 2004.

Hauerwas, Stanley. "Give Us Peace – But Not Yet." International Bible Advocacy Centre blog, March 23, 2021.

Hauerwas, Stanley. *Hannah's Child: A Theologian's Memoir*. Eerdmans, 2010.

Hauerwas, Stanley. *In Good Company: The Church as Polis*. University of Notre Dame Press, 1995.

Hauerwas, Stanley. *Matthew*. Brazos, 2006.

Hauerwas, Stanley. *Minding the Web: Making Theological Connections*. Cascade, 2018.

Hauerwas, Stanley. *The Peaceable Kingdom: A Primer in Christian Ethics*. University of Notre Dame Press, 1983.

Hauerwas, Stanley. "Peacemaking Is Political." *Plough Quarterly*, Spring 2021.

Hauerwas, Stanley. *Prayers Plainly Spoken*. InterVarsity Press, 1999.

Hauerwas, Stanley. *Sanctify Them in the Truth: Holiness Exemplified*. Abingdon, 1998.

Hauerwas, Stanley. *Should War Be Eliminated? Philosophical and Theological Investigations*. Marquette University Press, 1984.

Hauerwas, Stanley. *Truthfulness and Tragedy: Further Investigations in Christian Ethics*. With Richard Bondi and David B. Burrell. University of Notre Dame Press, 1977.

Hauerwas, Stanley. *Unleashing the Scripture: Freeing the Bible from Captivity to America*. Abingdon, 1993.

Hauerwas, Stanley. *Vision and Virtue: Essays in Christian Ethical Reflection*. University of Notre Dame Press, 1981.

Hauerwas, Stanley. *War and the American Difference: Theological Reflections on Violence and National Identity*. Baker Academic, 2011.

Hauerwas, Stanley, and Romand Coles. *Christianity, Democracy, and the Radical Ordinary: Conversations between a Radical Democrat and a Christian*. Cascade, 2008.

Hauerwas, Stanley, and William H. Willimon. *Lord, Teach Us: The Lord's Prayer and the Christian Life*. Abingdon, 1996.

Hauerwas, Stanley, and William H. Willimon. *Resident Aliens: Life in the Christian Colony*. Abingdon, 1989.

Hauerwas, Stanley, and William H. Willimon. *The Truth about God: The Ten Commandments in Christian Life*. Abingdon, 1999.

Hauerwas, Stanley, and William H. Willimon. *Where Resident Aliens Live: Exercises for Christian Practice*. Abingdon, 1996.

Stuart, Elizabeth, and Adrian Thatcher, eds. *Christian Perspectives on Sexuality and Gender*. Eerdmans, 1996.

Wells, Samuel, and Stanley Hauerwas. *In Conversation: Samuel Wells and Stanley Hauerwas*. Facilitated by Maureen Knudsen Langdoc. Church Publishing, 2020.

Plough Spiritual Guides

The Reckless Way of Love
Notes on Following Jesus
Dorothy Day

Love in the Void
Where God Finds Us
Simone Weil

The Prayer God Answers
Eberhard Arnold and Richard J. Foster

Why We Live in Community
Eberhard Arnold and Thomas Merton

The Scandal of Redemption
When God Liberates the Poor, Saves Sinners, and Heals Nations
Oscar Romero

That Way and No Other
Following God through Storm and Drought
Amy Carmichael

Thunder in the Soul
To Be Known by God
Abraham Joshua Heschel

The Inconvenient Gospel
A Southern Prophet Tackles War, Wealth, Race, and Religion
Clarence Jordan

Plough Publishing House
845-572-3455 ♦ info@plough.com
PO BOX 398, Walden, NY 12586, USA
Robertsbridge, East Sussex TN32 5DR, UK
4188 Gwydir Highway, Elsmore, NSW 2360, Australia
www.plough.com